GOLDEN YEARS
OF
PRESTON

The publishers would like to thank the following companies for their

support in the production of this book

Bako North Western Ltd

R Baron Ltd

W H Bowker Ltd

James Hall & Company Ltd

Kirkham Grammar School

Liquid Plastics Ltd

Tom Parker Ltd

Ribble Fuel Oils

T. Snape & Co. Ltd

Bernard Watson Decorators

Whittles Jewellers

First published in Great Britain by True North Books Limited
England HX3 6AE
01422 344344

ISBN 978 - 1906649081

Text, design and origination by True North Books
Printed and bound by The Amadeus Press

GOLDEN YEARS
OF
PRESTON

CONTENTS

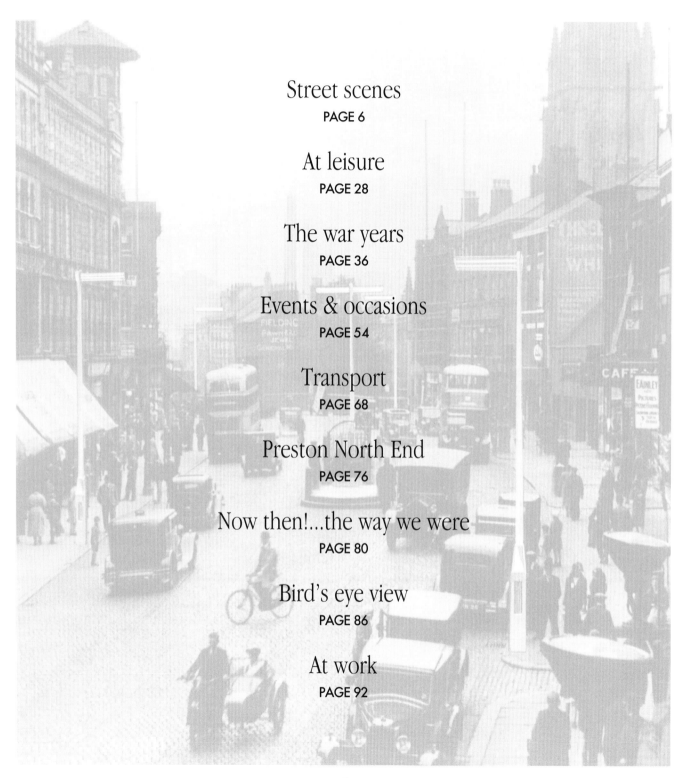

INTRODUCTION

In quiet moments we all sit back to reflect on the past. We dream of those days of yesteryear when everything seemed so much sunnier, when we were more content with life as it was. Perhaps we are fooling ourselves, but it is no sin to draw comfort from experiences through which we have lived or about which our parents told us.

It does help to have a prop to help and that is where 'Golden Years of Preston' will play its part. Within these pages is a wealth of nostalgia from 40 years ago and right back to the start of the last century. As the reader leafs through the book many half forgotten memories will come flooding back. Things that an older generation told us of will be there in black and white, firming up the mental images of a Preston that seemed to be locked into a time capsule out of our reach. The lovely photographs and accompanying text, variously informative, poignant and wry, help bring back to life a town and city that has changed so much as the years have unfolded. It is not just the buildings, skylines and thoroughfares that have altered but a whole way of life. The pace of the days when we were young or our parents were alive is recaptured within this nostalgic trip down memory lane. With the turning of each page will come a visit to Booth's store or Heaney's fish and game shop on Fishergate, a journey back to the Bond car works on Ribbleton Lane or a Saturday afternoon spent watching 'proud' North End, led of course by Tom Finney.

But it is not only the sights of the town that have changed. Even the vocabulary of the era that we examine in 'Golden Years of Preston' has undergone a transformation. Then we spent tanners, bobs and half crowns as we did our shopping. Everything was weighed out on scales that measured in pounds and ounces without fear of shopkeepers being prosecuted by our lords and masters in government who seem to regard metrication as a god to be worshipped. We ran up curtains by the inch, not the centimetre, and used words like 'please' and 'thank you'. 'Good morning' was a phrase used as we passed someone in the street without fear of being accused of harassment. Our children called neighbours 'uncle' or 'aunty', but now they are not spoken to because we do not even know their names. Mugging meant looking at someone's face, crack was a joke or a gap in the pavement and joyriding was a happy journey. But, with every hankering for the return of the old times and their values there must be some realism that it was not all days of wine and roses. There were also slum properties, areas of poverty and deprivation and the sheer horror of world wars that sent our brave lads off to the trenches and brought death and destruction raining down from the skies as enemy planes bombed our factories and homes.

As one of England's oldest boroughs, mentioned in the Doomesday Book, Preston was granted its town charter by Henry II in 1179 and rose to city status in the early years of this millennium. In the intervening time, it had developed as a significant port. By the 17th century, it paid more ship money in taxation to the crown than either Lancaster or Liverpool. As with most northern towns, the industrial revolution and the textile trade changed its face forever. A small market town became one with factories and smoking chimneys that dominated the Victorian skyline. There were some advantages in industrialisation. The founding of the Preston Gas Company in 1815 led to the lighting in our town being drawn from a source only then available in London. It was also one of the few early 19th century northern towns to have its own municipal borough council. The population was little more than 5,000 when that century dawned, but this figure had rocketed to a remarkable 125,000 by the time Queen Victoria was laid to rest. It has altered little since.

But, this book is not intended to be a dry and dusty history manual. Instead, it is a vibrant and lively homage to the years that moulded us, for better or for worse. So, why not get into the mood? Wind up the gramophone and put on a 78 of Dickie Valentine and his 'Mr Sandman'. Reach for a packet of Kensitas filter tips with their gift tokens inside and pour out a glass of foaming Corona cream soda. As Cilla used to sing, 'Step inside love'.

TEXT	ANDREW MITCHELL, STEVE AINSWORTH
PHOTOGRAPH COMPILATION	TONY LAX, ANDREW MITCHELL
DESIGNER	SEAMUS MOLLOY
BUSINESS DEVELOPMENT EDITOR	PETER PREST

STREET SCENES

The cars and buses on Church Street in the interwar years treated the entrance to the underground toilets as something of a traffic island. Down in the bowels of the earth, to use an apt if somewhat blunt reference, townspeople could quite literally spend a penny. That was the cost of opening the door to one part of the toilets. Ladies used to complain, with some justification, that this was another example of inequality as men could often use the facilities for free, but perhaps we ought to move on from this discussion before it becomes too basic. The type of conveyances rather than conveniences is an easier subject to consider. The handsome cars, all in black, jockeyed for position on the roads with the recently introduced buses. A couple of cyclists happily swung across the scene in the foreground as a real period piece headed towards the camera. The motorbike and sidecar was a popular mode of travel. It was also potentially hazardous as there was little in the way of protection should rider or passenger be involved in a major accident. There was little consideration given to the wearing of protective headgear. Perhaps the driver might don something like a flying helmet and the passenger a flat cap or headscarf, but that was about it. In the days when there were AA and RAC patrols on the road, many used motorcycle sidecars. The riders would salute a member as their paths crossed. It was a nice touch of old world respect.

At about the time that the Edwardian age came to an end in 1910, the view from Friargate across Market Place showed off Preston's architectural centre in all its glory. The Harris building, Miller Arcade and former Town hall (pictured bottom right) were magnificent examples of 19th century planning and design.

The acclaimed Grade 1 Listed Harris Museum & Art Gallery sits proudly in the centre of Preston, dominating Market Square.

The idea of creating a free public library and museum had been championed in Preston, since the 1850s when members of the community began holding fund-raising events. However, it was not until 1877 that a bequest by the Preston lawyer, Edmund Robert Harris made the idea of a free library, museum and art gallery a reality. He left £300,000 to Preston Corporation in memory of his father, the Reverend Robert Harris, who had been vicar of St George's Church for 64 years. The sum was to be split equally to build the Harris Museum, the Harris Institute and the Harris Orphanage.

The Harris Library, Museum and Art Gallery was designed by James Hibbert, a local architect and Alderman of Preston. He was born in Preston in 1831 and educated at

Above: A fine view of Preston's magnificent old Town Hall. The building which stood between Market Square and Fishergate was built in the 1860s and was designed by Sir George Gilbert Scott, leading architect of the Gothic Revival. The Cloth Hall in Ypres, in Belgium provided Scott with his inspiration. It was considered to be one of the most beautiful town halls in Great Britain. Tragically, it was destroyed by fire in 1947.

Preston Grammar School. Hibbert used the Greek Revival style for the design of the new building, to portray the high cultural standards achieved by the Ancient Greeks, which he felt were most suitable to reflect 19th century ideas and attitudes. This differed markedly from the Gothic Revival Town Hall designed by George Gilbert Scott. To prevent a clash of styles, the building was set on the western side of the square, adjacent but not next to the old Town Hall. The foundation stone was laid in 1882 by the Duke of Lathom as part of the Guild Celebrations for that year.

The Boer War memorial on the left was a shortlived addition to this vista. The obelisk was designed by T Hodglinson. Mounted on a pedestal with a two-step base, it

was unveiled on 6 October, 1904, by Major General Kekewich. It was paid for by funds raised by public subscription. Inscribed with 86 names, it gave homage to the sacrifice of those members of the Loyal North Lancashire Regiment who lost their lives in the South African campaign, known as the Boer War. The memorial was moved to Avenham Park in 1919 when plans were considered for a memorial in this square that would honour those killed in the Great War.

Left: Interior view of the Miller Arcade, an elegant Victorian building with its Italian terracotte facade modelled on the Burlington Arcade in London

Below: The cobbled setts on Church Street at the junction with Derby Street had little in the way of traffic with which to contend in early May 1937. The streets were already decorated in anticipation of the celebrations that were to be held to mark the crowning of George VI as our monarch. In faraway London, the pageantry and excitement of the day could only be transmitted over the radio airwaves to the rest of the country. Loyal subjects had to wait until newsreel footage brought images of the procession to Westminster Abbey onto our cinema screens before getting a glimpse of the scene. How different it would be when the next coronation came along. That whole ceremony was transmitted to the nation by BBC Television, prompting households to rush out and purchase their own little black and white sets in the early summer of 1953. In this photograph, the steeple of the parish church rises above the garlands and streamers. Originally, the church of St Wilfrid occupied this site, but it was demolished, replaced and renamed as St John's in the 16th century. The parish church was the first in the whole country to benefit from gas lighting when the first flame was lit in 1816. Two years later, the Preston Gas Company threatened to cut off supplies for non payment of bills! In 1853, the church was subjected to major rebuilding.

Above: The scene across Market Place shows the Harris Library, Miller Arcade and Town Hall. The photograph dates from 9 May 1937, just three days before the coronation of George VI. The square would be filled with revellers when that special day arrived, but the celebrations were somewhat muted within the heart of our new monarch. He was a reluctant king. Prince Albert, Duke of York, as he was when his brother succeeded their father, was thrown into the spotlight after the abdication fiasco of late 1936. Albert hated the limelight and, as a nervous and diffident man who suffered from a speech impediment, knew that being under public scrutiny would be nerve wracking for him. But, he had to do his duty, unlike his selfish brother. The buildings in view are some of the most imposing you could wish to see. The former Town Hall that stood on the edge of Fishergate was destroyed by fire in 1947. This was a loss to the city as the fine edifice was one of G G Scott's finest creations. Built in the 1860s and inspired by the Cloth Hall in Ypres, it was one of the best examples of Gothic revivalism that you could see. Miller Arcade was modelled on London's Burlington Arcade and has a delightful terracotta façade. However, pride of place goes to the Harris, the mixture of museum, library and art gallery that was designed by James Hibbert and completed in 1893.

Above: There really was a time when the motor car did not dominate the highways. None of us can recall those days, so we have to rely upon photographic evidence, as in this one of Church Street. The trams would have clattered along the lines, but many people used their own feet to get around. It was also a time when the bicycle was heavily employed. With great advances in tyre manufacture, allied to the introduction of such helpful devices as the three speed Sturmey Archer gear in the early 1900s, two wheeled travel boomed in popularity. The pastime was a relatively cheap and cheerful way to keep fit, as well as offering an alternative to travelling on public transport. The isolated bicycle on the left is an additional reminder that we are looking at another age. Imagine leaving such a piece of equipment unattended today.

Below: Kirkham Street is to the north of the city centre, just off Fylde Road that can be seen at the top of the photograph. Many of the houses in this part of Preston were built to provide homes for those working in the textile industry, especially at Moss Mill, built for John Horrocks in 1796. Pictured in 1935, these dwellings were among the most poorly equipped in the town. Those living in the cellars and basements had it particularly tough as they were gloomy, dank and smelt of damp almost all of the time, however hard families tried. It comes as no surprise to learn that incidence of respiratory illnesses was high and living here became something of a vicious circle. Kirkham Street was home to those who did not have sufficient means to break free from the chains of poverty and the accompanying scourge of ill health with which it seemed to go hand in hand. Even those posing for the camera were hard pushed to look anything other than woebegone. Preston embarked on a programme of slum clearance in the late 1930s and several thousand council houses were built, but the outbreak of war put the programme on hold. It was not resurrected until the mid 1950s when estates such as The Larches, at Ashton, and developments at Middleforth Green, Brookfield and Penwortham were begun.

Below: With Harrops, Edwards and Victoria Carpets on the left, this view shows Friargate as it was in 1962. The east side property opposite Lune Street was earmarked for demolition as the new ring road was built. The swinging 60s was a decade of change. The coffers in the nation's town halls were full and those empowered to do the spending were ready and waiting to get started. New roads had to be built as the rise in family motoring put strains upon our overloaded transport systems. Slum clearance and the building of new estates needed completion and there were town centres to be remodelled. The man in the street had money to burn as well. The economy was booming after the austere years of most of the previous decade. There were young people out there as well who had voices that demanded an ear. They were born during the savage wartime years and, with the later addition of their younger siblings, the baby boomers, there was a sort of revolution in the air. They would not accept the standards and attitudes of their parents. After all, who wanted more wars and aggression? Angry young men were writing and producing gritty literature that told it as it was. The popular music was no longer moons and Junes, but hard nosed rock instead. Those who thought that privilege meant power were in for a nasty shock as teens and twenties flexed their financial muscles.

Above: The former Town Hall was badly damaged by a fire in 1947. Herman Goering's Luftwaffe had filled the skies with bombers in the early 1940s, but our seat of local government had remained unscathed, only to perish in peacetime. Here it can be seen in a forlorn condition, prior to demolition. Built in 1862, it provided an attractive and imposing presence in between Fishergate and Market Place. There is something impressive about council chambers that were built in Victorian times. The very architecture lends a sense of the sombre and the meaningful to proceedings that are conducted in such surroundings. Modern buildings and the rooms and offices used may be much lighter and more airy, but they lack that majestic atmosphere given by the high ceilings and ornately carved, decorative plaster and stonework provided by architects who were around over a century ago. As these locals went about their business in these early days after the last war, they knew that there was much rebuilding to be done. This did not just mean bricks and mortar, but a restructuring of a society that had taken us into two world wars in just a matter of a few decades. It was for this reason that voters decided in the summer of 1945 to dispense with the services of Winston Churchill and his brand of politics. We gave Clement Attlee, full of ideas about nationalisation and the welfare state, the chance to run our affairs. Time would tell if we were right.

Above: The shops on the corner of Corporation Street and Kendal Street were soon to be demolished. The pedestrian crossing is a period piece as there are no carriageway markings, other than the studs that guided a pedestrian over the road. The black and white design with which we are so familiar and the description 'zebra crossing' did not materialise until the early 1950s. The beacons were named after Leslie Hore-Belisha who was the Minister for Transport when a raft of safety measures was introduced in an effort to improve standards on our roads. Our record in terms of fatalities and accidents in proportion to the number of vehicles and miles travelled on the highways was among the worst in Britain. Better education on road safety for pedestrians, cyclists and motorists was introduced. The Highway Code was published and driving tests became mandatory for new drivers. More electrically controlled traffic lights were introduced, roads had Percy Shaw's cats' eyes fitted and pedestrian crossings were installed at dangerous points. Having done his bit for road safety, Hore-Belisha had moved to the War Ministry two years earlier when his crossing was photographed in 1939. He stayed as Secretary of State until being sacked in 1940 after falling out with Prime Minister Chamberlain and several Cabinet colleagues. He lost his parliamentary seat in the 1945 Labour landslide to an up and coming new kid on the block called Michael Foot.

Below: The bobby in the centre of the tram tracks was asking for trouble as his attention does not seem to have been firmly fixed on the traffic sneaking up behind him. Perhaps his fancy was taken by the vivacious looking young woman in the very modern 1920s' style of cloche hat and short skirt. If that is where his gaze was headed, then she could literally be described as a bobby dazzler. Back in the 1960s, our television viewing included two American series that had their action centred upon that previous period of flappers and gangsters. 'The Roaring Twenties' starred Dorothy Provine as Pinky Pinkham, a singer in a fictitious New York nightclub, The Charleston. 'The Untouchables' was even more popular. Starring Robert Stack as Eliot Ness, it told of the Chicago police force's attempts to clean up the city during the days of Prohibition. No such problems were found on Fishergate as we look to the right at Edward Dewhurst's electrical engineering shop. This company was founded at 89 Fishergate in 1887 as a telephone engineering concern, before branching out into a wider electrical market. Dewhurst's later moved to Mount Street and now has its headquarters at Anchorage Business Park in Ashton-on-Ribble. Very much a family firm, the founder's grandson is now the chairman and two great grandsons are joint managing directors.

Some photographers need more than a camera to carry out their chosen profession. In this instance, a head for heights was also de rigueur. Nerves of steel and a steady hand were additional requirements as the intrepid soul mounted the roof of the Harris Library in 1936. Looking beyond the war memorial in the foreground takes along Friargate. On the horizon we can see many factory chimneys belching out their fumes into the sky above. The various Clean Air Acts of the early 1950s and the decline in the textile and traditional manufacturing industries helped improve the environment. It was in need of all the help it could get as, before the last war, the north of England was a mucky place to be. Yet, as they say in Yorkshire, where there is muck there is brass. It was thanks to the prowess and inventiveness of people like the locally born Richard Arkwright that we had an important industry on our doorstep. In the 18th century he developed a spinning frame that produced a thread far stronger than anything else available. It was able to spin 128 threads at a time. As it did not need a skilled operator to run it, the Arkwright frame could be used by the humblest of workers. Dozens of mills were built from the late 18th and through the 19th centuries. By 1900, some 80 per cent of Preston's population was linked with the textile industry for its livelihood.

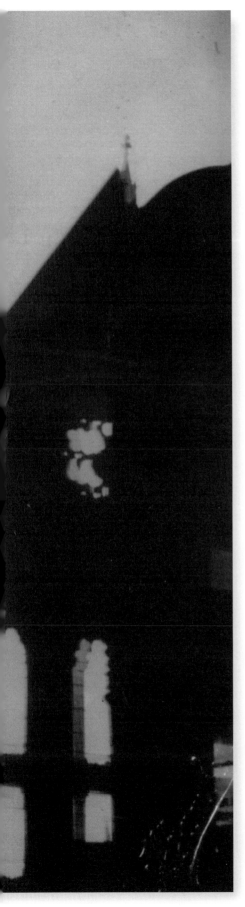

There has never been a definitive answer about what or who caused the Town Hall fire in 1947. The fire brigade had no time to wonder about the background. There was the here and now to deal with. The men on the turntable ladders carried out their jobs with professionalism, but it seemed to onlookers that they were fighting an unwinnable battle. The flames rose high into the night sky and their hoses seemed to be providing just a trickle of water in comparison with the intensity of the conflagration in front of them. At least they had more chance than the first organised firefighters seen in Preston. They had little more than a large barrel of water on a wagon, but

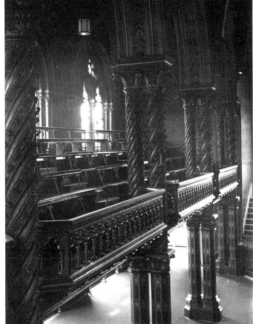

the contraption was the forerunner of the modern fire appliance when it was first used in the town in 1724. Although things became a little more sophisticated over the subsequent years, a large leap forward did not occur until a steam powered fire engine was pressed into service in 1872. Firemen often went about their work wearing the sort of large, ornamental helmets that were eventually only ever seen on ceremonial occasions. The introduction of electricity into factories and homes meant that the combination of water and metalwork on a person's head was a risk not worth taking when fire exposed cables and bared wires.

Right: With plans well under way for the building of St George's Shopping Centre, we know that it must be about 1963 as we look at the former entrance to A E Roberts and Company. St George's was opened as a brand new experience for Preston's shoppers, but has attempted to modernise itself in more recent times with trendy name changes to The Mall St George and then just The Mall. Older shoppers stick to the name from the swinging 60s. The entrance used to lead to Harding's stables. Many of the horses here had the job of pulling cabs and trams in the late 19th century. They had long been put out to grass when the centre was built. Now it was

the age of the motor car and the hoarding over the head of the shopper with her typical basket bellowed that there would be ample space to park up and shop for those who drove into town. That attitude would change as the end of the century approached. By then, one way systems, no entry signs, parking restrictions and pedestrian only areas were the order of the day and the car had become something of a pariah. Park and shop gave way to park and ride.

Above: The Central Police Station and combined Magistrates' Courts on Lancaster Road opened in 1858. They are both now on Lawson Street. In early Victorian times Lancashire was one of the most crime ridden parts of the country. One local resident was so moved by the situation that he wrote to the Preston Chronicle in early 1840 complaining of the 'midnight work of plunderers, burglars and wanton and maliciously disposed persons'. He would have been pleased to note that the newly-formed Lancashire Constabulary was in the act of recruiting a force that would number 660 men by the end of the following year. They had their work cut out as the local press reported that the 'bobbies' or 'Peelers' in some towns were the object of organised assaults. During that first year officers were attacked by colliers in Middleton, beaten up by drunken mobs in Lancaster and set upon by rioters in Colne. A policeman's lot was not a happy one, as Gilbert and Sullivan would later confirm. Things were more settled in 1965 when this scene was captured on film. In this year Parliament decided to abolish the death penalty, leaving Gwynne Evans and Peter Allen with the unenviable record of being the last men to have been hanged in Britain. Shopping

Left: Looking along Lune Street towards Friargate in 1960, two old pubs occupied opposite sides of the road. Drinkers in the Corporation Arms on the left could look across at those enjoying a pint in the Spread Eagle Hotel on the right. St George's Shopping Centre, that opened in the mid 60s, now dominates the east side of this area and Friargate and beyond is now largely pedestrianised. Although we gained a bright and new set of retail outlets when St George's was built, to be followed by the mall on Fishergate 20 years later, we lost so much of our heritage and way of life. Like the baddie in the story of Aladdin offering new lamps for old, we were seduced by the glitz provided by the town planners.

Above: Fishergate, at the junction with Chapel Street, was almost as busy with traffic in 1955 as it is today. As part of the one way system. The photographer was facing towards Market Place and would now be looking at St George's Shopping Centre to the left. There are now traffic lights on the corner where Henry Dodgson's store once dominated. This place was a cut above the rest, or so it tried to infer. It was not just an outfitter's, but a costumier and furrier, according to the lettering on the façade. Of course, wearing a fur coat or stole was something to which up-and-coming people wished to aspire. Lady Docker, the wife of Sir Bernard, chairman of the Daimler car company, was just the sort of person who attracted such hopes and ambitions. She was originally Norah Collins, one time dancer at the Café de Paris. The desire for release from austerity was nowhere more evident than in the public's fascination with this publicity seeking couple. The pair entertained the nation with a succession of fancy cars, mink coats, champagne receptions and their magnificent 860 ton yacht. It was not to last as Sir Bernard lost his job in 1958 and the pair went to live in more humble surroundings on Jersey as tax exiles. The Dockers never shopped at Hodgson's, though they might have approved of the upmarket range offered by Swear and Wells clothing.

Below: The Preston Industrial Institute for the Blind was founded in 1867. This was largely thanks to the work of John Catterall who had, for several years, used a cottage in which he taught a small group of blind men the craft of basket weaving. From this small, but most worthwhile, venture grew a larger organisation that was able to offer greater opportunities to the visually challenged. They were also afforded a sense of dignity in that they could contribute meaningfully to their own welfare, rather than merely relying on charity or the support of family and close friends. New premises on Glover Street, off Avenham Lane, were opened in 1874, enabling the work to be expanded. Thomas Seholefield, himself a blind person, became the manager of the Institute in the late 19th century and served in this capacity until his death in 1912. In 1895, buildings on the Cottage Home principle,

costing £8,000, were opened in Fulwood. By now, people were including bequests to the institute in their wills and, in 1923, an additional home, the Roper Hostel, was established at Fulwood. In 1930, there were 537 blind people on the register, with 19 accommodated in the Institute Hostel. Retail outlets, like this one on Lune Street's east side pictured in 1960, provided a source of income from the sale of goods manufactured by the blind. Dewhurst's the butcher occupied the adjacent site for many years. Once owned by the Vestey family, this firm was a familiar name on most of Britain's high streets. But, mounting competition from supermarkets saw its demise in 1995. It was relaunched in the 2000s with limited success and went once more into administration in 2006. George Banks' jeweller's is still at 31 Lune Street, next to the old Redfern's shop.

on their first house. They would then put the money down as a first payment on a building society loan that would get them onto the first rung of the housing market. Older savers used their accounts to squirrel away cash towards their next car or their first foreign holiday, while others used the interest on their deposits to top up their pensions. It was such a simple way of doing things in 1960. Later, ordinary people and big business both got greedy. The societies became banks and the public wanted the good life today at yesterday's prices. When tomorrow dawned, there was not enough cash in the pot and crunch time was with us. Preston Gas Company Offices were in use before they became those of the North Western Gas Board. The building belonged to the company that first saw life in 1815 and was incorporated in 1839. The foundation stone for these offices was laid on 14 October 1872. They were demolished in 1965.

Above: Fishergate Baptist Church dominated the street's skyline in 1881 in this peaceful scene. This palindromic year saw the formation of the Union of Baptist Churches taking place on 26 January. The religious movement dates back to the early 17th century when two radical ministers, John Smyth and Thomas Helwys, conducted a baptismal ceremony in Holland with which they attempted to display that their brand of Anglicanism was completely without any connection with Catholicism. The first Baptist Church was founded in Britain in 1812 and is now the fifth largest Christian sect. Members were referred to as 'nonconformists' and one of their main tenets was that Christ was the head of their church, not the monarch. In 1881, as these Preston shops opened for business horses ambled along, pulling carts and traps behind them.

Right: The Halifax Building Society, on Fishergate, was one of a clutch of places from where we once could get a mortgage. Owned by its own members, young people invested their hard earned money in such societies and let their savings build up until they had sufficient to make a deposit

Below: By 1980 Preston had experienced a number of changes on its streets over the previous two decades. These were largely centred on the alterations to traffic flow and the redesigning of the town centre area to accommodate the provision of shopping malls. On the pavements we could also see changes in the people who passed us by. There was a greater number of people whose family roots were in Asia, notably India and Pakistan. On Fishergate, it was becoming less and less of a novelty to see a pretty lady in a sari or shalwar kameez. Men in turbans above pin striped suits were just as likely to turn the corner as those wearing yarmulkes on their heads. We were becoming a cosmopolitan society. Food in the shops echoed this with mango chutney sitting side by side with HP sauce on the shelves. By the late 1990s, Corner Shop's 'Brimful of Asha' with Tajinder Singh on vocals would top the singles' charts.

AT LEISURE

Avenham Park is a delightful place in which to forget the cares of the world for a while. It is also a spot where large crowds have gathered on important and celebratory days, such as the Preston Guild, festivals or royal coronations. The parkland was the brainchild of landscape gardener Edward Milner (1819-94). He was fortunate in that he served an apprenticeship at Chatsworth under the guidance of the master craftsman of his day, Joseph Paxton. Milner went on to become the Superintendent of Prince's Park, Liverpool, and later fulfilled a similar role at what is now Crystal Palace Park, Sydenham. He then set up in business as an independent designer. Milner worked in Buxton and Lincoln, as well as a spell abroad in Denmark. Avenham Park was created close to the Ribble in a natural wooded amphitheatre and is less formal than the adjacent Miller Park that Milner also designed. He used the riverside walk that was established in the late 1840s as the starting point for Avenham. Consideration for the aesthetic appeal of the area had already been given when it was decided that the railway along the west side of the site should have ornamental bridges and an avenue of trees. Land was purchased for the park by the Corporation in 1852 and the grounds and gardens were laid out in 1861.

Above: Hell may not have frozen over but the Ribble certainly did in 1940. These jolly skaters were happy to escape the wartime blues for a while and enjoy a simple pastime. In the background, the bridge once belonged to the North Union Railway. This company was formed in 1838 by an amalgamation between the Wigan Branch and Preston and Wigan Railways. At that time the line ran from Preston to Warrington, via Wigan where it connected to the Liverpool to Manchester route. After Stephenson's Rocket made its pioneering run, a proliferation of small railway companies were formed. Many only lasted a short while before amalgamating with or being swallowed up by other enterprises. The North Union, itself a joint venture, survived in isolation for a few years. By 1846 it was part of the Grand Junction and Manchester and Leeds Railways. This became even more complicated as it evolved into the London and Northwestern Railway (LNWR).

Below: The Living Union Jack and the Red Rose of Lancaster were the subjects of this display. The historical pageant was into its third day on 9 September, 1922, and the general theme was a celebration of the British Empire. We still had one in those days, but it was starting to creak a little at the seams. The world map had large chunks coloured in red, but this was not going to be the case for evermore. But, who would have thought that we would lose not only our colonies and many of our dependencies but also our influence on the world stage in a matter of just a few decades? We all knew that the great Victorian times were behind us, but at least we still ruled the roost in places where hardly any of us would ever dream of setting foot. At the time of the Preston Guild celebrations that we see here in Avenham Park, our colonies ran alphabetically from Aden to Zanzibar and in population numbers from the 318 million in India to the 200 souls to be found on Ascension Island. The British ruled vast tracts such as the 3.5 million square miles of Canada to the miniscule two of Gibraltar. It was truly the Empire where the sun never set.

Right: The Hoop and Crown was one of the hostelries that called Friargate its home. It is seen here looking in a rather sad and sorry state just before it was demolished in 1938. This photograph helps preserve the memory of those bygone days that are not part of our own immediate memories as they belong to a time that our parents or grandparents experienced. Fortunately for us, the Preston Scientific Society was a forward thinking group and, in 1937, formed a committee responsible for creating a photographic record of the changing face of the town. Given the task of maintaining memories of disappearing landmarks, this branch of the Society kept itself busy for about a quarter of a century in compiling many volumes of photographs that are still in use as part of the Local Studies section of our city library. The Hoop and Crown was a good place for theatregoers to enjoy a tipple before nipping into the Royal Hippodrome next door. After the pub was pulled down the Coronation Chambers were built here. Among the new businesses was one that might evoke a few memories. A dancing school, firstly the Worsley and later called the Halford, was established on this site. Ballroom dancing was a necessary social skill that the vast majority of people mastered in the middle of the last century.

Left: Friargate's Royal Hippodrome opened in 1902. Theatres, variety shows and music halls were hugely popular for a night out. Live entertainment was in demand a century ago, but tastes change and the call for pre-recorded material increased as time went by. This was particularly illustrated by the way in which the nation flocked to the cinema when that became widely available. Places such as the Hippodrome continued to offer alternative entertainment for a while, but their days in staging live shows were numbered. The writing was definitely on the wall after the last war. The variety show with pretty dancing girls opening proceedings, followed by a singer, magician, an animal act, a comedian and a top musician, were on their way out. Straight plays were acted out in front of empty seats. Leonard Rossiter, a young stage manager who would become a well known TV star, worked here in the early 1950s. He said that he was always anxious that not enough would be taken at the box office to fill his weekly pay packet. The demolition notices were pasted up in 1958 and the building was flattened the following year. The C and A department store was then built on the site. The spout on Slinger's ironmonger's shop, to the right, has been preserved and can be seen in the city museum.

Left: The Theatre Royal stood on Fishergate. The original building was erected here in 1802 and many famous thespians trod its boards before extensive alterations took place in 1882. In addition to dramatic presentations, stars of the music halls performed here on a regular basis. In the last century it opened its doors to the cinema loving fraternity. In 1955, one of the last movies it showed before closing its doors for good was one that helped change the course of popular entertainment. 'Blackboard Jungle' was a fairly routine melodrama set in a slum school starring Glenn Ford and featuring an up and coming young actor in Sidney Poitier. . The storyline was not the sort that any 12-year-old could have written as good guy teacher turned naughty pupils into angels. Instead, it was one that actually tried to deal with the subject of teenage angst. Additionally, behind the credits the voice of a dumpy man with a kiss curl on his forehead was heard singing a tune that would help mould a generation. 'Rock around the clock' was ignored by audiences at first, but word spread on the teenage grapevine. Soon, the movie was attracting a younger clientele that started dancing in the aisles and tearing up seating as it seemed to go into a frenzy as it embraced the new sound. The rock 'n' roll era was born. The Theatre Royal was demolished in 1956 and was replaced by the ABC cinema, though that as well is no longer with us.

Right: If you are not aware of your place in society, then you are now. This railway poster, dating from about 1900, was a clear message to those who got their hands dirty for a living that the Irish Sea had been reserved for them as from next Sunday. Until then, of course, and on other days of the week, it seems to imply, such unsavoury ruffians as the working classes had to remain on the shoreline. Although it is hard to believe that the coast would be policed by constables on the lookout for people in flat caps or pinnies above their bathing cozzies, the poster is a true refection of the attitudes of the management classes. They regarded themselves as a cut above the rest, albeit a notch below the landed gentry who were above all criticism or limitation. The cost of rail travel suggested that the working classes who were invited to take to the waters had a few bob in their pockets. These were no knock down prices. Two shillings from Preston to the seaside is only 10p in modern money, but it was more than a day's wage to the man in the street over a century ago.

Seen from Central Pier in about 1905, the beach and promenades at Blackpool attracted millions of visitors each and every year. The mill towns of Lancashire closed their doors for a fortnight each summer and the holidaymakers packed themselves into railway carriages to enjoy their bit of freedom from drudgery during their Wakes' Weeks. They promenaded along the Golden Mile munching on fish and chips, bought kiss me quick hats and squealed with a mixture of delight and fear as they took a ride on the Big Wheel. But no time spent in Britain's premier resort was complete without a visit to the Tower. At the time of this image it was still a relatively recent attraction as it only opened on 14 May 1894. The idea for this tourist attraction came from a visit to the 1889 Paris Exhibition by Blackpool's Mayor, John Bickerstaffe. Impressed by the Eiffel Tower, he encouraged businessmen in his home town to fund a similar structure, Designed by Maxwell and Tuke, it cost a whopping £290,000 to build. It was not painted properly and had to be rebuilt in the 1920s when corrosion threatened its existence. The Tower Ballroom opened in August 1894 and was immediately popular. In 1930 Reginald Dixon became the resident organist. He was still playing 'Oh I do like to be beside the seaside' when he retired 40 years later.

THE WAR YEARS

Below: The captured German Army field gun was put on display in Market Place in 1916. The 7th Battalion of the Loyal North Lancashires was formed in 1914 and saw active service in Europe. Included in its involvement was the Battle of Loos in northern France that saw the first use of the new army units known as 'Kitchener's Army'. The first salvoes were fired on 25 September 1915. Initially, the British had considerable success, easily breaking through the enemy lines and taking the small town of Loos-en-Gohelle and acquiring various artillery pieces, including this field gun. Our troops deployed chlorine gas during the battle, but with mixed success. The wind changed and blew clouds of the noxious stuff back into our faces. The gas masks were inefficient and some soldiers also removed them as the eye pieces clouded over. Those who were sent back from the front lines to recuperate were sworn to secrecy in case morale was adversely affected. The early successes were soon more than cancelled out. A failure in the supply chain and a lack of communications led to troops being exposed to machine gun fire across open ground. By the fourth day, our boys were back where they started, but 20,000 of their number lay dead. Among them were Rudyard Kipling's son, Jack, and Fergus Bowes-Lyon, brother of the future wife of George VI.

Right: Oh what a lovely war. Men from the 4th Battalion of the Loyal North Lancashire Regiment had landed in France and were ready to go and do their bit for king and country. There are some famous names included among the battle scars of this

battalion as its members participated in the Battle of Festubert in 1915 and then on the Somme, the Ypres salient and Passchendale. It was also involved in the breaking of the Hindenburg or Siegfried Line in 1917. The men looking towards the camera were in a jolly mood. However, their optimism and joy would be short lived as they came face to face with the stark reality of trench warfare. In the 19th century, battles were no longer fought using frontal assaults as improvements in the range and accuracy of firearms had made such a style quite suicidal. So, the stalemate of warfare in the trenches replaced the cavalry charge. But, the conditions in them were such that if a stray shell or bullet did not get you then disease or an infected wound would do so instead.

Left: D Company of the 7th Battalion of the Loyal North Lancashire Regiment was known as the 'Preston Pals'. Seen at Preston Railway Station on 7 September 1914, these men were looking forward to an adventure on the continent in the service of their country. 'We'll be back before you know it,' they remarked to wives, sweethearts and mothers. These pals were typical of many such groups up and down the country. At the start of the war, in early August, the government decided to recruit an extra 500,000 men to serve the country's fighting personnel needs. Lord Kitchener, the Secretary of State for War, was one of those who felt that this conflict needed millions and not thousands of conscripts and volunteers. He drafted the famous 'Your country needs you' slogan and set about urging men to enlist in droves. General Henry Rawlinson, one of the leading army chiefs, came up with the idea that men would be more likely to sign up if they could do so with people that they already knew. The idea of the Pals' Battalions was born. Relatives, workmates, friends and neighbours all rallied to the cause. However, when they were pitched into battle at such places as the Somme, the far reaching effect of the wholesale slaughter of such groups was horrendous. With communities decimated and families mourning losses, often of more than one member, the experiment was not repeated at any future date. As one Pal put it, the experience was two years in the making and ten minutes in the destroying'.

Above: The whole street turned out on a day that was both sombre and uplifting. Heysham Street was a road like any other, filled with terraced housing. However, the family at No 7 was something special. On 31 August 1916, it stepped across its threshold to greet both pride and sadness that had come to call. This was the home of Private William Young, a native of Glasgow who had served as a regular soldier before taking up employment at Preston Gas Works. He re-enlisted in 1914 in the 8th Battalion of the East Lancashire Regiment. He was gassed in 1915, badly damaging his eyesight, but he made a gradual recovery and eventually returned to action. Back in the trenches on 22 December 1915, he saw a wounded sergeant lying in no man's land. Without a thought for his own safety, Young braved enemy fire and went out to reach the man. Despite being hit twice, he carried him back to safety. He was awarded the Victoria Cross for this conspicuous act of gallantry. Sadly, there was no happy ending for Bill Young. His injuries required a series of operations over the subsequent months, though he seemed to have rallied in April 1916 when he attended a civic reception held in his honour at Preston Town Hall. Unfortunately, he suffered a relapse and died on the operating table three months later. His old regiment formed the guard of honour at his funeral. Private Young's medals are now on display at the Duke of Lancaster's Regimental Museum.

On 19 November 1914, Lord Derby addressed a huge crowd in Market Place. Standing on the Town Hall steps, close to Miller Arcade and the Crown Hotel, he was issuing a rallying call for men to enlist and join the war against Germany that had been declared three months earlier. Initially, going off to the front was seen as something of an adventure. There was even talk of it all being over by Christmas and no-one really expected the spat with Germany to be much more than a falling out between friends. It was nearly a century since Waterloo, the last major engagement by British troops in Europe. The bumping off of some Archduke in the Balkans seemed inconsequential to

those of us living in Bamber Bridge or Fulwood. The first British action of the war took place in Belgium and involved a few shots and sword cuts inflicted by a cavalry regiment. How that pattern of assault would change. Within a couple of months, major battles at Mons, Arras, the Marne and Ypres would be under way. Those at home started to get an inkling that this was not going to be the 'jolly' that we anticipated. Edward Stanley, the 17th Earl of Derby, was a powerful orator. He was the figurehead of the recruitment campaign for Kitchener's Army and the government gave him an official title as Director General of Recruiting. He became the Secretary of State for War in 1916.

Above: The ceremony of returning the colours to the Loyal North Lancashire Regiment was held in Market Place on 6 December 1918. The large gathering acknowledged the service that the soldiers had given and three loud and lusty cheers rang out across the square in front of the Town Hall. The Regiment was formed in 1881 as part of the restructure of the British Army and was based at Fulwood Barracks. The initial two battalions were expanded to 21 during the First World War. They served on the Western Front, at Gallipoli, in Macedonia, Palestine, East Africa and Mesopotamia. Some 7,590 casualties were suffered during these campaigns and three Victoria Crosses were won. It was again expanded in World War II to a total of 10 battalions. They served in North West Europe, Malaya, North Africa and Italy. On 25 March 1970, it amalgamated with The Lancashire Regiment (Prince of Wales's Volunteers) to form The Queen's Lancashire Regiment.

Below: It was rather late in the war, though they did not know it at the time. On 22 June 1918, the recruitment parade was held along Fishergate, crossing the railway bridge with County Hall in the background. Volunteers were sought for the Women's Land Army (WLA) and these members urged their sisters to join up and do their bit for the war effort. Most of us are aware of the work done in the fields by land girls during World War II, but their mothers had performed similar, but less publicised, duties a quarter of a century earlier. With up to 6 million men serving in the armed forces, Britain struggled to fill the places they had vacated on the shop floor and on the land. The Board of Agriculture organised the WLA, beginning activities in 1915. Many traditional farmers were antagonistic to the idea, but government advisers were sent out to speak to them and encourage their co-operation. In truth, there was no alternative. By the time of this parade in Preston, some 250,000 women were enrolled as farm labourers, tilling the soil, haymaking, working on animal husbandry and keeping the food chain well supplied. Many women were reluctant to return to traditional female roles after the war as a further blow for emancipation had been struck.

Tank Week began in Preston began on 21 January 1918. 'Egbert' was one of the travelling or presentation tanks of the Lincoln class that toured the country in the latter years of the Great War. When the general public saw Mark IV tanks for the first time during the Lord Mayor's Show in London in November 1917, it was amazed at this new wonder machine. Six of these were sent on tour, like some modern day pop star, spending a week in a town as a sales pitch for war bonds and war savings certificates. Given sturdy sounding names, 'Egbert', 'Old Bill', 'Julian', 'Drake', 'Iron Rations' and 'Nelson', they attracted crowds who marvelled at the advances made in modern technology. When the war began it was the horse that seemed to be the most important means of getting around, but now we

had lorries, cars, motor ambulances and these fighting machines that moved across impossible terrain. During Tank Week residents were made to feel as if they had a personal stake in the one that stood in their town square. Although most of these travelling tanks stayed in Britain and were solely used for advertising purposes, Egbert had seen active service. It was one of those used in the Battle of Cambrai in November 1917 when General Sir Julian Byng was ordered to relieve pressure on the French lines. The offensive consisted of an attack against the Germans' Hindenburg line along a 10-mile front. The chosen terrain, rolling chalk downs, was especially suitable for tank movement. Over 300 of these vehicles smashed through German defences and some 7,500 prisoners were taken at low cost in casualties in the first assault.

With the Post Office, Municipal Building and Session House in the background, the Armistice Day remembrance service was held on 11 November 1935 in front of the War Memorial. Civilians and those in uniform joined together to pay homage to those who died during what was then known as the Great War. It had been regarded as the war to end wars and, if the full lessons of the immense carnage wreaked had been learned, so it should have been. But, despite the tears shed and the memories evoked at ceremonies such as this one, man continued to injure, maim and kill his fellow human beings. 'Lest we forget', the inscription says, but we did and all too quickly.

Left: In the late 1930s, as the outbreak of war seemed a certainty, civil defence groups began organising their strategies and trained members in the use of measures that would help combat the effects of modern warfare on the civilian population. The issuing of gas masks and instruction in their use was one such measure. Newsreel footage from the Spanish Civil War emphasised that hostilities would include the bombing of industrial centres and cities and could possibly involve the use of gas and other noxious chemicals. All schoolchildren were issued with them in the early summer of 1939 and they carried them in purpose built boxes to and from lessons. At the start of September 1939, any youngster being evacuated from the major urban areas clutched a battered suitcase in one hand and a gas mask in the other. Babies also had special helmets into which mothers would have to pump air with a bellows. Even the police were expected to don the less than flattering apparatus, but it was a wise precaution even if the fear of a gas attack never materialised.

Above: Air raid shelters were part of the nation's defences against the attacks by German bombers during the last war. They came in a variety of shapes and sizes, from large basement areas in municipal buildings or at underground stations to purpose built affairs that were constructed on waste land or in someone's back garden. The smaller ones for individual family use were first seen in 1938 as people began to prepare for the possibility of war. Designed by William Paterson and Oscar Kerrison, this type was named as the Anderson Shelter after John Anderson, the Lord Privy Seal, who had responsibility for air raid precautions. The basic design was of corrugated, galvanised steel panels that formed a structure sunk about four feet into the ground. This was then covered with soil or sandbags. Some streets and parishes even had competitions for the best shelters as families grew flowers and vegetables in the surrounding ground. Anyone earning less than £250 per annum received a free Anderson, while the better off were charged £7. Over 2 million were issued during the war. In towns and cities targeted by the Luftwaffe, the nightly vigil in the shelter became commonplace and they were often quite well equipped with the essentials. When peacetime came many households turned their shelters into garden sheds or re-erected them on an allotment.

Above: During the last war there were frequent salvage drives. It was a waste not, want not culture and full of suggestions about making do and mending. Raw materials were scarce and anything that could be recycled was put to use. Those of us in the 21st century who think of ourselves as being 'green', and of being among the first to counteract the throwaway society, should look back to the 1940s. Here, children collected all sorts of stuff that could be turned into something useful. Anything from an old envelope to a garden rail was collected and transported to a sorting centre. There, armies of volunteers sifted and graded rags, bones, paper, metal and any other items that could be put to further use. Throughout the war years appeals for junk and salvage were ongoing. Sometimes we were asked to hand over old saucepans, flat irons and bedsteads to provide scrap metal for the building of new warships and planes. It seemed ironic that the Spitfire overhead might really be a flying frying pan. Not to worry, as long as it did its job. The British, weaned on a diet of jumble sales and white elephant stalls, were past masters (and mistresses) at scavenging. The skill was to serve them well.

Right: Pictured is a passing out parade of the East Lancashire Regiment at Fulwood Barracks. The East Lancashire Regiment was formed in 1881 as part of the Cardwell reforms of the British Army. It was formed initially with two battalions, the 1st Battalion being created from the former 30th Regiment of Foot, and the 2nd from the former 59th. The first Regimental Depot was in Burnley, but moved to Fulwood Barracks, Preston in 1898.

On 1 July, 1958, the Regiment amalgamated with the South Lancashire Regiment to form The Lancashire Regiment (Prince of Wales's Volunteers), which in 1970 in turn amalgamated with The Loyal North Lancashire Regiment to form The Queen's Lancashire Regiment. Fulwood Barracks has throughout its history been the main focus of military activity in the county, and has often had wider regional responsibilities. Before the Second World War, HQ 42nd (East Lancashire) Division was stationed here. More recently, HQ North West District moved into the Barracks in 1976 and, in 1991, HQ 42 (North West) Brigade re-formed at Fulwood and became the regional military headquarters for North West England. The Barracks also houses the HQ and training facilities of the Lancashire Army Cadet Force. Fulwood Barracks was the last and largest of a chain of barracks built in the North West in the wake of the Chartist riots of the 1830s. Not only is it now the sole remaining example, it is today the finest and most complete example of mid-Victorian military architecture left in the country.

Above: 'What are you doing, mister?' This warden was using the telephone box as a handy resting spot as he filled out some return or checked a particular detail on his log of events. He was a member of the Air Raid Precautions (ARP) team of civilians who offered their services as volunteers on the home front. Many were in jobs that had a protected status as their work expertise was invaluable to wartime production. Others were too old or unfit to join up, but still wanted to play their part. There was also a small handful who just enjoyed being officious and belonged to what came to be known as the 'jobsworth' mentality. Such a type was admirably portrayed by Bill Pertwee as Warden Hodges in the BBC sitcom 'Dad's Army'. During the blackout, cries of 'Put that light out' and 'Don't you know there's a war on?' were often mimicked by comedians as part of their variety acts, but most wardens played an important role during the grim days of the early 1940s when we were under attack. They were often in the thick of it, assisting the general public find shelter during an air raid. They also reported the extent of bomb damage and assessed the local need for help from the emergency and rescue services. The wardens used their knowledge of their local areas to help find and reunite family members who had been separated during an air raid.

Below: During World War II all sorts of essential and non-essential foods were rationed, as well as clothing, furniture and petrol. Before the Second World War started Britain imported about 55 million tons of food a year from other countries. After war was declared in September, 1939, the British government had to cut down on the amount of food it brought in from abroad and decided to introduce a system of rationing. People were encouraged to provide their own food at home. The 'Dig for Victory' campaign started in October, 1939, and called for every man and woman to keep an allotment. Lawns and flowerbeds were turned into vegetable gardens. Chickens, rabbits, goats and pigs were reared in town parks and gardens. Ration books were issued to make sure everybody got a fair share. They contained coupons that had to be handed to the shopkeepers every time rationed goods were bought. Food was the first to be rationed. On 8 January 1940, bacon, butter and sugar were rationed. Clothing rationing began on June 1, 1941. There was a shortage of materials to make clothes. People were also urged to 'Make do and mend' so that clothing factories and workers could be used to make items, such as parachutes and uniforms, needed in the battle against Germany. Every item of clothing was given a value in coupons. Each person was given 66 coupons to last them a year. Later it was reduced to 48 coupons. Children were allocated an extra 10 clothing coupons above the standard ration to allow for growing out of clothes during a year. This did not prevent children having to wear 'hand me downs' from older brothers and sisters. In a make do and mend environment, trousers and skirts were patched and darned, old jumpers were unpicked and the wool used to make new garments. Rationing continued even after the war ended. Fourteen years of austerity in Britain ended at midnight on 4 July, 1954, when restrictions on the sale and purchase of meat and bacon were lifted.

Below: It was something to talk about at school tomorrow. This was part of the march past along Lancaster Road that was held on 13 May 1945. The Victory Parade celebrated the end of a war that had been officially concluded the week before. However, although the street parties had been held and the processions had wound their way along the streets, this was only victory in Europe. For many families, the waiting was not over. There were still thousands of our brave boys who were missing, suffering in Japanese POW camps or still fighting though the jungles of the Far East. It would be another three months before Emperor Hirohito would finally wave the white flag of surrender. Some of the little tots watching this parade would never see their fathers again, for they lay on some foreign field or beneath the waves. Others would eventually greet men who were almost strangers into their homes; it being so long since they had last clapped eyes upon them. This caused strain on many households and a lot of those coming back felt rejected rather than welcome. The strain on many a marriage told and divorce levels hit new records in the late 1940s. Not every demobbed serviceman felt like a returning, conquering hero.

Right: They are notorious for both their accuracy and their worship of the cult of populist celebrity, but television polls are cheap to organise and the results are easy viewing. One such show of recent years looked at the list of the greatest Britons and actually concentrated on people who did something worthwhile. So, instead of Robbie Williams or Katie Price topping the poll, we got such divers contributors to greatness as Brunel, Thatcher, Newton and Shakespeare. Pride of place, though, went to Winston Churchill. Although any such award is subjective, it cannot be denied that he had a great influence on 20th century Britain. Pity the offspring who had to walk in his shadow. Randolph Churchill (1911-68) had to carry the cross of having a famous father. Seen here in uniform on 25 September 1940, he

was handing in his nomination papers to Mayor W E Morris to become Preston's Member of Parliament. The sitting member, A C Moreing, had died and a by election was called, though Churchill was eventually returned unopposed. He represented the town until 1945, but lost his seat in that year's Labour landslide. Despite having served with distinction during the war and becoming a journalist of some note, he was always resentful of his father's greater fame. His bad temper and heavy drinking became the stuff of tabloid headlines, but many felt that he was often portrayed in an unfair light.

Bottom right: The Yanks said a thank you to us for our hospitality and we showed our own gratitude to them for their commitment to helping ensure that those bluebirds could fly over the white cliffs. The

victory parade along Lancaster Road was held on 13 May 1945, just five days after we had heard the announcement on the radio that the last shots had been fired in Europe. For locals, there was something of a togetherness with our American cousins after that dreadful day in the nearby village of Freckleton. On 23 August 1944, a B-24 Liberator overshot the runway at the USAAF airbase at Warton while attempting a landing during a violent storm. It ploughed into the village, demolishing several houses, flattened the local C of E primary school before coming to rest in a snack bar ironically patronised by American servicemen. Some 38 schoolchildren were killed, along with 23 adult

civilians and air force personnel. Both the host and visiting communities were greatly touched by the tragedy and an affinity between them still exists. A memorial garden and children's playground was opened in August 1945, with a stone tablet bearing the inscription 'This playground presented to the children of Freckleton by their neighbours of Base Air Depot No. 2 USAAF in recognition and remembrance of their common loss in the disaster of August 23rd 1944'. Shortly after the disaster a visit was paid to the area by the singer and film star Bing Crosby. He was visibly moved by what he heard and saw. However, although local people knew all about the event, it was not until after the war that the full facts were made available to everyone.

EVENTS & OCCASIONS

The Flag Market in front of the old Town Hall and Harris Museum is the original, historic market site. It has often been used in more modern times to stage a variety of events and activities. Hence, there can be specialist markets, followed by fun fairs and even ice skating taking place. It is also a focal point for prestigious events such as proclamations and remembrance services. The Flag Market was regarded as the heart of the city, but redevelopment in the 1960s and the creation of shopping malls meant that the west side of the area enjoyed more interest. The building of St John's Centre and the bus station also provided something of a dividing wall with the rest of Preston. That was long after locals enjoyed themselves during the 1902 Preston Guild. On the far side of the square, Friargate leads away. Franciscan friars, or Greyfriars because of the colour of their habits, arrived in Preston in 1260. The friary was closed in 1539 during Henry VIII's purge of monasteries and sold to a Thomas Holcroft. Friargate was subjected to a street widening programme in the final decade of the 19th century, along with the entrance to Market Street, over to the right. The 1902 Guild celebrations looked forward to life in the last century of the millennium, with a newly crowned king in Edward VII on the throne.

Below: The butcher's float, complete with its own cow, was part of the Trades' Procession in the 1902 Preston Guild celebrations. The decorated floats and the marching accompaniments were a glorious sight as they bowled along Fishergate. People hung precariously out of windows or over balconies in order to get a better view. Those in charge of the floats had spent days beforehand in making sure that everything was just tickety boo for the great day. The wagon was carefully prepared and the horses well groomed. The brasses were so highly polished that you could see your own reflection in them. Everything had to be just so because you were representing your trade, profession, church, society and so on. Not only that, but get it wrong and you had 20 years to wait before a chance of redemption would present itself.

Top right: Men raised their hats in homage to the royal couple and women shouted their hurrahs in support of King George V and Queen Mary. They strode out along Stanley Street purposefully as they honoured one of the town's most famous employers. Horrocks' Mill was a most important part of the local economy and this was acknowledged when the visit was made on 8 July 1913. At that time, the royal house was known as Saxe Coburg-Gotha because of the line back to Prince Albert, King George's grandfather. Queen Mary, formerly Princess Victoria Mary of Teck, had been engaged to George's brother, but he died of pneumonia in 1891. Her affections were transferred to the future king almost by royal decree when Queen Victoria made it clear that she approved of a match between a grandson and the Princess. At the time of this photograph, the royal family's standing with the general public was at a low level. Kaiser Bill and the German nation were not the flavour of the period and this was to become much worse in the months leading up to the outbreak of the Great War. To have family links with the enemy was to court unpopularity and possible insurrection. George and Mary made their loyalties clear in 1917. The royal house was renamed Windsor, German titles were dropped and others anglicised. The Russian revolution later that year showed just what could happen if the masses became alienated from their monarch.

Below right: Princess Victoria Alexandra Alice Mary was known to everyone as Princess Mary. Born in 1897, she was the only daughter of the eventual King George V. Her first state appearance was made at he father's coronation in 1911. Despite her youth, she took a keen interest in the plight of wounded servicemen during World War I. To this end, she visited many hospitals and involved herself in projects that lent assistance to the injured and their families. Her Christmas Gift Fund raised large sums as well as numerous presents that could be sent to the front and give soldiers and sailors some home comforts and, better still, the knowledge that they were not forgotten. Towards the end of the war, Mary took a nursing course at Great Ormond Street Hospital. She also developed a keen interest in the Girl Guide movement. She became that association's president in 1920, a position she would retain until her death 45 years later. Seen on 6 August 1929 in Market Place, the Princess showed a pretty ankle as she inspected the honour guard of Guides. By now she was also Viscountess Lascelles, having married the future 6th Earl of Harewood in 1922. Having first lived at Goldsborough Hall, the couple made their home at Harewood House, one of Yorkshire's finest stately homes and estates.

Above and right: Views of Church Street decorations in 1902 from the corner of Miller Arcade and the Guild procession on 5 September 1922. The garlands and streamers festooning the streets along the way made an attractive backdrop to the celebrations. The group in the centre of the pictured on the right belonged to the Catholic Guilds and represented the faith that has always been particularly strong in this part of the world. Known in some quarters as 'the Catholic capital of Britain', Preston's links with the church can be seen in a probable derivation of the city name. 'Priest's town' is not too far a jump from the modern spelling. The lamb depicted on the city crest is a biblical image of Christ as the lamb of God or agnus dei. This animal is also representative of St Wilfrid, our patron saint. The letters 'PP ' at the bottom of the crest stand for 'Princeps Pacis', prince of peace, though some would have you believe that it means 'Proud Preston'! Although largely committed to Catholicism, other religions have had a considerable presence here over the years. In 1837 the Mormons began preaching here in their first foray outside the USA. Links with the area were maintained and a huge temple was built by the Church of Jesus Christ of Latter Day Saints, as it is more correctly known, at Chorley in 1998. Preston also has a number of evangelical churches and, in more recent times, has seen a growth in followers of Islam and Hinduism.

Above: On your marks at the starting gate and ready for the off. With Deepdale soccer ground behind them, this group of riders was about to participate in a torchlight procession as part of the 1922 Preston Guild Merchant celebrations. The origins of the festivities go right back to medieval times when an organisation or guild of traders, craftsmen and merchants controlled the town's economy and business. It established a regular review of its activities and meetings were held in 20 year cycles, thus laying down the basis for the time scale we have today. The saying 'once in a Preston Guild', meaning not very often, has become part of the English language, especially in the north of the country. Although the Guild's powers waned over the years as administrative affairs were later controlled by town councils, the celebratory and festive aspects of the meetings were retained. There is some dispute over the year in which the first event was held, but most believe it to be in 1328. However, the 20 year pattern was not properly established until 1542. From then on the rule was observed religiously until 1942 when no celebrations were held because of the war. They were revived in 1952 and the traditional two decade pattern began all over again.

Above and below: In the last century we were well used to seeing kings and queens visiting us, but they were usually called Edward, George or Elizabeth. The royal personage getting a special reception at Horrocks'

Mill on 19 July 1927 was King Fuad of Egypt. There had long been connections between the major European powers, notably France and England, with Egypt during the 19th century. This was made all the more important after the opening of the Suez Canal in 1869. After the First World War, the Egyptians tried to throw off the yoke of European influence and revolution against foreign rule was the order of the day. Britain finally acknowledged the country's independence in 1922. Sultan Fuad had become the leader of Egypt and Sudan in 1917 on the death of his brother. He assumed the title of king five years later but struggled to keep control of his country as the nationalist Wafd Party flexed its political muscles. The twice married Fuad had other problems in that both his marriages were unhappy ones. After his death in 1936, his second wife sold all of his clothes to a local used clothes market trader in revenge. Their son, Farouk, became King at the age of 16. After the last war, he was a frequent visitor to Europe, earning a reputation as a spendthrift playboy. He became so unpopular at home that he was deposed in 1952 and, a year later, the monarchy was abolished.

Below: Mardale village in the Lake District disappeared in 1935 when the Hawes Water reservoir was created and the valley was flooded. It was done to provide a collecting point for water from the nearby hills and streams that could then be pumped to homes in Manchester. That city's Mayor and a party of 70 councillors made a special visit to view the project and entered the Mardale tunnel in a series of railway tubs. Despite the uncomfortable nature of the ride and the damp conditions that they were about to experience, these local bigwigs looked to be quite a cheery group. The woman in the foreground was a most attractive looking soul who would win our vote any day of the week. The visiting party were the guests of Manchester Corporation Waterworks and wore protective clothing that had been supplied by Attwater and Sons, a Preston company founded in 1868 in Bluebell Yard, Church Street. The buildings in Mardale village were blown up by the Royal Engineers, who used them for target practice. Alfred Wainwright, the noted authority on walking in the Lake District, was just one of many who voiced disapproval. Traces of the old village can be seen during periods of prolonged dry weather when the water level falls sufficiently.

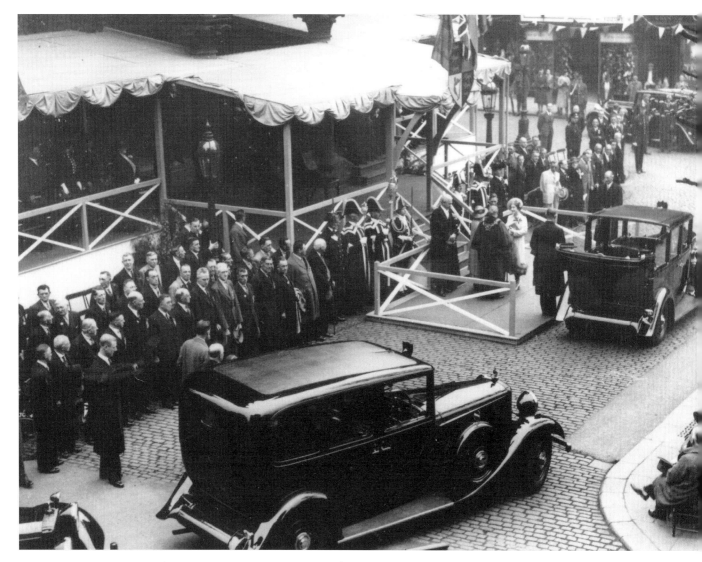

Above: A neatly draped canopy was erected outside the Town Hall to provide attractive protection from the vagaries of an English spring for the dignitaries who assembled on 17 May 1938. Rows of attendants in ceremonial garb and lines of councillors and other officials attended the Mayor as he wished King George VI and Queen Elizabeth a fond farewell as they concluded their visit. The limousines in the motorcade arrived to take the royal party on to its next stop. The cars had their period stylishness and were typically 1930s. The spare wheel carrier on the side, the adjacent door handles and the running board were common features that were part of the action in television's 'The Untouchables'. The series, popular in the 1960s, told of America's battle with its gangster culture. However, there was no chance of Legs Diamond or Babyface Nelson appearing with a machine gun in the centre of Preston. The car carrying the King and Queen was an open top tourer, giving crowds a good view of their majesties. It was inconceivable that such a well loved couple would be a security risk.

Right: It was all pomp and circumstance on Church Street as the procession celebrated Mayor's Sunday on 6 November 1936. It was unlikely that the liveried pair out in front had just left Dunn's outfitters as that company dealt in more practical men's garb. This day has long been a regular event on the civic calendar. The mayoral role has its roots in the royal charter granted to the town by King Henry II in 1179, though the first recorded mayor, Aubrey son of Robert, was not in office until 1327. Today, the position is usually filled for just a year, but in the past there have been many instances of people being re-elected year after year. Reuben Ainsworth, in the late 1940s, was the last to serve consecutive terms, though William Beckett was in office on two separate occasions in 1946 and 1965. Ernest Ley was the incumbent in this photograph. He was a diminutive figure, but was highly respected because of the importance of the office he fulfilled. His regalia included the chain that was purchased with a public subscription of £800 in 1887 to mark Queen Victoria's Golden Jubilee. Designed by Alfred Gilbert, it was first worn by Mayor James Burrow in 1888. Preston was a forward looking town when, in 1933, it elected Avice Pimblett to be one of the country's first female mayors.

Below right: The 1930s was the decade of swings of fortune and a diversity of moods. It began with unemployment on the rise and a general feeling of malaise in the country as successive governments failed to make good the pledge to build a Britain fit for heroes after World War I. As the era unfolded, more and more were out of work and, by the end of the decade, we were embarking in another global conflict, just over 20 years since peace had been declared for its predecessor. Yet, we had some national celebrations that centred upon the royal family. Then we were able to let our hair down and enjoy the festivities that were arranged for us. The first of these took place on 6 May 1935 when George V had his silver jubilee. The biggest crowds since Armistice Day in 1918 flocked onto the streets. Four generations of the royal family attended a service at Westminster Abbey and scenes like this one at Avenham Park were repeated across the nation. The park, along with neighbouring Miller Park, opened in 1867. Designed by Edward Milner, a former apprentice to Joseph Paxton of Chatsworth

fame, Avenham is host to a number of historical structures, including the Belvedere, Swiss Chalet, the Boer War Memorial, the railway viaduct and the Japanese Gardens. There would be more royal celebrations two years later when George VI was crowned.

Above: On 12 May 1937, hordes of children from local elementary schools were treated to an afternoon's 'field day' celebrations as part of the festivities held in honour of the coronation of King George VI. They flocked into Avenham Park and enjoyed the entertainment provided for them. Elementary education was the name used to describe the learning provided for children attending publicly funded schools. They would later be called 'council schools' or 'county' ones. Developed from the 1870 Elementary Education Act, these establishments were sometimes called 'industrial schools' in their early days as they were largely set up to cater for the needs of the working classes in towns and cities. Education focused on the three Rs, with some attention to training in manual activities, as appropriate to gender needs. Girls learned housecraft and boys practised woodwork. The school leaving age was set at 14, though at first family budgets often demanded that youngsters did not stay the full term. Children attended an all-age school and it was not until 1944 that a new Act provided for three progressive tiers of education: primary, secondary and further. The kiddies in the photograph enjoyed the Fred Astaire lookalikes on the stage. 'Top Hat' was one of the best grossing movie musicals of the period and the song and dance man was in his prime. It was an era when elegance was important and style meant something.

Below: It was the summer of 1938 and it was just over 12 months since our new king had been crowned in Westminster Abbey. Being a shy and retiring man, he was not well known to the general public. After all, it was his elder brother who had hogged the limelight and the face of Prince Albert, Duke of York, was only splashed across the front pages following the abdication crisis of late 1936. Having become King George VI, he and his wife, Queen Elizabeth, embarked on a 'getting to know you' tour of the country. Unlike her predecessors, this doughty lady was not satisfied with playing second fiddle as a mere consort. Not only did she regard her marriage and position as representing a partnership, it was the former Elizabeth Bowes-Lyon who often took the lead. This was partly through choice, but partly through necessity. Without her drive and, at times, protection, her nervous and tentative husband would have had difficulty in coping with the public demands of his position. During this nationwide tour, the royal couple spent four days in Lancashire. They lunched at County Hall on Tuesday 8 July, having been given a marvellous reception in Market Place by the bandsmen of the 4th Battalion of the Loyal (North Lancashire) Regiment who provided a rousing rendition of the national anthem. Here, the couple is seen leaving, on the way to Moor Park to meet representatives of the British Legion.

Left: Little boys used to have knees. They disappeared somewhere in the late 1970s when primary schools stopped insisting that they came to lessons dressed like children. Instead, they were allowed to wear all manner of long trousers. Little girls were also condemned to become young women when ankle socks and dresses were phased out in favour of jeans, denims and track suit bottoms. On 6 February 1928, there was no doubting that these lads were properly turned out, just like lads should be. Their shoes were well polished, collars and ties smartly in place and jackets neatly brushed. They had already inspected Preston's town regalia and were now having a good look at the official charter. The Town Clerk had given an address to the boys about Preston's history and they were happily browsing among the documents and Town Hall trappings. This was part of the Rotary Club boys' civic week, a programme designed to make youngsters more aware of the workings of local government. It is interesting to note that girls were not considered to be worthy of inclusion in the project. That was not surprising as it was only in this year that their mothers finally got full voting rights in parliamentary elections. Rotary clubs were established so that local businessmen could put something back into the community.

Right: Taken from a helicopter hovering above Avenham Park, this aerial photograph of the 1972 Preston Guild shows the Children's Pageant in full swing. The involvement of youngsters on any large scale was largely a 20th century innovation. In earlier days, the Guild merchants, law makers, landowners and influential businessmen and administrators used this as a demonstration of their authority. This was also a way of advertising to a world beyond the Preston boundary the importance, power and sophistication of the town itself. The most influential and well established Lancashire families always attended and would never appear unless dressed in all their finery. With the reformation of the Corporation in 1835, the Guild celebrations gradually became part of the life of ordinary men and women. Churches and schools began to participate, top entertainers were invited to appear and plays with well known actors were produced. There were regattas on the river, firework displays and much merriment instead of the pomp and circumstance of previous occasions. The railways brought visitors from far and wide who enjoyed the historical

themes of the pageants that the kiddies mounted. Many a little boy cherished the silver cardboard armour and wooden sword, along with a colourful, flowing cloak and fancy papier-mâché helmet, that mum provided him with for his part as a Roman legionnaire.

Bottom left: Councillor Joseph Hood, Mayor of Preston, bowed deeply in honour of his guest, Queen Elizabeth II. The Duke of Edinburgh, as was always the case, took up a deferential position several feet behind his wife. This had been his lot in life for a quarter of a century and would continue to be so for another 30 years and more. He had been prepared for it somewhat during the four years that he was married to a princess. It is to his credit that he has served the country and his wife as the most noble and blameless of consorts. In 1977, there were national celebrations to mark the Queen's Silver Jubilee. Street parties had echoes of VE Day and the Coronation as the country let off steam and showed its support for the monarchy. The royal couple's visit to the Town Hall, with the Guild Hall in the background, was just one stop during a nationwide tour of the country. Preston folk showed how proud they were by turning out in droves on 20 June.

Below: The hemlines on the young mums in this photograph, as they helped the Miles Street children tuck into a jolly spread, gives us the year of this particular Preston Guild party. It just had to be 1972. The very tiny micro minis of the late 1960s had become that bit more decent, especially when bending over to serve the next glass of orange juice. Hot pants were all the rage for a little while in the early 1970s, but women can be fickle followers of fashion. Before long the midi and then the maxi skirt had their moments. The kiddies did not worry about modern trends or current fads. They were just happy that the sun was shining and that they could party.

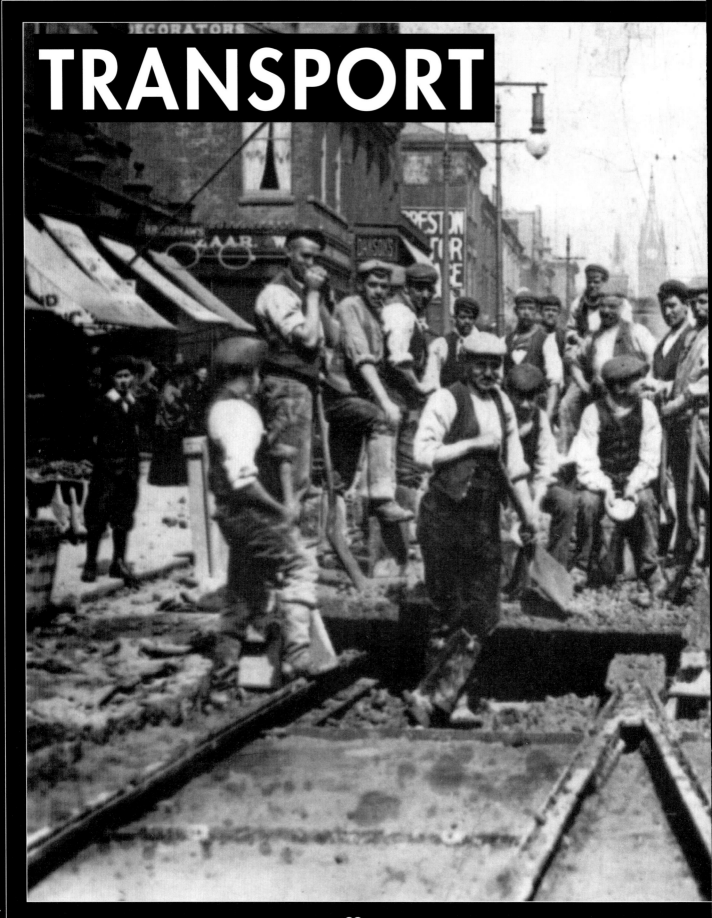

TRANSPORT

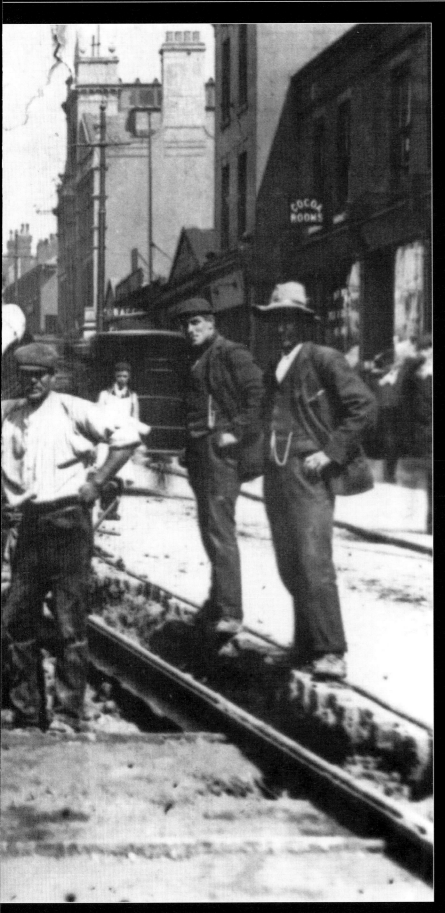

These labourers were close to completing the laying of the new tramway on Fishergate for the electrified service that went into service in 1904. Horses first pulled the tramcars from Fishergate Hill to the Pleasure Gardens at Farringdon Park, near the cemetery, in 1882 and another service from the Town Hall to Ashton commenced at about the same time. There was also a daily bus service to Higher Walton and weekly ones to Goosnargh, Walmer Bridge and Much Hoole. But, with the introduction of the electric tram, the face of public transport was changed forever more. There were 14 miles of track laid in and around the town and there was talk of extending it to link in with Lytham and Blackpool to the west and Blackburn and Horwich to the east. In the end, these ideas were not enacted. Some towns imported tramcars from America, but we had our own company based in a factory on Strand Road. Dick Kerr was an electrical works formerly based in Scotland. It moved south of the border and built more trams in its time than any other British firm.

Below: No wonder the old dear on the top deck wore her largest and warmest piece of headgear. It must have been a draughty ride for her. Sitting on hard wooden benches was not the most comfortable of rides, but ally that with the wind whistling around your ears and the sooner the driver got this bus under way, the better she would be for it. If she was going all the way to Chorley, via Whittle le Woods, from Station Road in Bamber Bridge then she had a seven mile journey to endure. In 1909 she could have knitted half a cardigan in the time it would have taken to complete the trip. That is if she could have kept her hands steady as the bus leapt along on boneshaking wheels that transmitted every bump in the road or uneven cobblestone through to the passengers. The link bus was owned by the Lancashire and Yorkshire Railway Company and was used to connect travellers with the stations at Chorley and Bamber Bridge. The lads in front of the bus made an interesting fashion statement. They were dressed just like dad. With their flat hats, waistcoats, shirts and breeches they looked more like little men than children. Towards the back of the bottom deck, a little girl peeks through the window. With her bonnet and bows, she has a childlike appearance, but not so her male cousins outside.

Right: Horse drawn trams served the town for the best part of half a century. Richard Veevers, a wealthy Quaker from Fulwood, established a route from near to his home into the town centre in 1859. This inaugural service did not prosper and only lasted for about 12 months. It did, though, inspire others to have a go. A more reliable service was maintained

between Ashton and Preston and the Preston Tramway Company re-established the Fulwood connection by building a new track to there in 1879. This extended from Lancaster Road to the old Prince Albert Hotel, now The Sumners, on Watling Street Road. The introduction of an electric tramway in 1904 killed off the horse drawn service. The one we see here was the very last to run. Snapped near Fulwood Barracks, the final journey was made on 31 December 1903. It was not a happy new year for the horses as they lost their jobs, but perhaps they had some retirement to which they could look forward. The driver had to learn new skills so that he could get to grips with the technology of the time. There was also new terminology to master, such as 'pantogram'. This was the name of the arm that connected the tram and its motor to the electricity running through the overhead cables.

Right: This Wolseley was manufactured in about 1904 and was one of the earliest vehicles owned by James Hodson. From 1910, he ran a taxi and small bus service that included a route from Gregson Lane, in the Hoghton area, to Preston. The Wolseley was developed by a firm that was originally the Wolseley Sheep Shearing Company. Among its early managers was a certain Herbert Austin. He was to go on and found his own successful motorcar empire. The first four wheeler that Wolseley built was sold in 1901 and the company expanded by taking over

Siddeley Autocars. Rebranded as Wolseley Motor Company in 1914, it developed links with North America and the Far East in the interwar years. It was bought out by William Morris, though the company name was retained on models that were produced right up to 1975. By this time the name was in the hands of British Leyland. Oddly enough, the sheep shearing business is still going as Wolseley plc. James Hodson's vehicle was purchased in 1919 by the newly formed Ribble Motor Service Limited. It was to become the largest bus operator in the northwest and one of the largest in the country. The red coachwork on the buses was to be seen operating services from Carlisle to south Lancashire. All good things come to an end and the company was absorbed into the Stagecoach Group in 1988.

Above: The very first electric tramcar got under way on 7 June 1904. Preston Corporation tramways proudly celebrated the occasion at the corner of Lancaster Road with Church Street. This inaugural car was full to bursting, but health and safety issues were for a later generation to fuss over. The earliest trams were pulled by horses and later powered by steam on the Swansea and Mumbles Railway that first ran as long ago as 1807. The Americans soon picked up on the idea and developed their own streetcars, as they called them. New Orleans in Louisiana still has a service that first saw the light of day in 1835. Rather bizarrely, it was not the mighty Americans or the inventive British who were the first to electrify their tramways. The honours in such pioneering ventures went to destinations on mainland Europe. Budapest saw the earliest electric tram in 1887, while the first regular service was established in Sarajevo in 1895. Helsinki's electrified network, opened in 1900, is probably the oldest one in the world to have had continuous use.

Below; All aboard the Skylark. This could almost be a scene from Nutty Noah and Niggly Nelly's popular television series for children in the early 1970s. There is just a slight flaw in that fanciful notion as the people featured in this posed photograph are from a decade that was much earlier. The last Penwortham tram ran from Liverpool Road on 4 July 1932. The route was taken over by motor buses and the passing of the age of tramcars was obviously celebrated with great gusto.

Whether this represented affection for the old or delight at the new, then the jury is still out on that one. Whichever it was, there were many happy, smiling faces on show. The first electrically powered trams ran in Preston on 7 June 1904. This inaugural route went from Lancaster Road to the Barracks on Watling Street Road, via North Street. The route was extended a month later to run back past the Deepdale Road depot and into the town centre.

Above: Author Kenneth Grahame (1859-1932) is best remembered for his 1908 book 'Wind in the Willows'. The driver of this 1933 car might just have been modelled on Mr Toad. It is certainly the type of tourer that would have got the old boy's heart racing, as well as the engine. He would happily speed along the lanes, shouting 'What fun!' and fun it must have been in real life for the owner of such a car. Britain's roads were not cluttered with traffic as they became later on and it was easy to find an open stretch of road and just let rip. Younger readers might look at the front of the car and observe a small hole at the bottom of the radiator grille and wonder as to its use. This was where a starting handle was inserted and the engine cranked over if the so called self-starting button or interior switch did not succeed in stirring the car into life.

Right: In 1965, the old Ribble Bus Station, on Tithebarn Street, was where many an out of town reveller arrived for a Saturday night on the tiles. This was the time of the swinging 60s and new dance clubs and night spots opened, with live music played by local bands. Visiting groups, particularly from the vibrant Merseybeat scene, cut their teeth in these venues and at the Top Rank dance hall on Fishergate. There was still a balance between old and new styles, as the hit parade of the time would testify. Ken Dodd with 'Tears', The Seekers' 'The Carnival is Over' and Roger Miller's 'King of the Road' all topped the charts, as did The Beatles, Rolling Stones, Hollies and Unit 4 Plus 2. Dance halls and resident bands still offered the chance to practise the quickstep and waltz, but these were about to become passé as girls danced round their handbags, often without the need for boys to accompany them. Then, it was back to the bus station for the last one home. The Ribble company dominated public transport on the northwest's roads during most of the last century. It was absorbed into the Stagecoach group in 1988. In this photograph, the tower of the former Sessions House can be seen on the left. Built in 1903 in a neo-baroque style, it was extended in 1933 and later became the Town Hall.

Right: The driver and conductor of this 1934 Preston Corporation double-decker bus take a well-earned break before continuing on their route to the Town Hall.

PRESTON NORTH END

Established in 1881, PNE was the first club to win both league and the FA cup, having achieved the noteworthy double in English football's inaugural season in 1888/89. Preston became known as 'The Invincibles' as they powered on through the entire season without losing a game, a feat only matched by Arsenal more than a hundred years later in 2003/04. Over the years the clubs fortunes have been mixed, with major honours in top flight football being limited to the league championship in 1890 and the FA Cup in 1934. The team has however, achieved success as champions in the lower leagues by winning titles in 1904, 1913, 1951, 1971, 1996, and 2000.

There were plenty of crowds about in early May 1937. The crowning of a new king was to take place on the 12th of the month and this inspired thousands to come onto the streets in celebration. Nine days earlier, similar numbers filled the square outside the Town Hall to welcome home Preston North End's soccer team. It was back from Wembley where it had played against Sunderland in the FA Cup Final 48 hours earlier. From the evidence presented in this photograph you might think that the lads had lifted the trophy, but no such luck. Despite taking the lead just before half time, thanks to a Frank O'Donnell goal, our opponents were inspired by the magical Raich Carter and scored three times in the second half to leave Preston hearts broken. The cup

was presented to the Sunderland skipper by Queen Elizabeth. Unlike modern soccer sides, the 22 players on the pitch that day came from just two countries. England had 10 representatives and Scotland 12. North End returned to Wembley in 1938 and emerged victorious with a much changed team. Only Andy Beattie, Bill Shankly, Len Gallimore and Hugh O'Donnell played in both finals. A civic reception was held for the lads who had performed so well against one of the top sides in the land. It had been good to get back in the public eye, and to honour the players efforts. The great days of the late 19th century were behind us and a losing appearance

in the 1922 FA Cup Final was all we had to look back on in the 1900s. Mayor James Harrison and his fellow council members claimed some of the reflected glory by inviting the boys onto the Town Hall balcony from where he addressed the large crowds in Market Place. You would have thought that he had devised the tactics as he waxed lyrical about the wing half play of Milne and Shankly. Politicians just love to bathe in the limelight surrounding the sporting achievements of others. Remember 1966? Harold Wilson won the World Cup for us, not Geoff Hurst or one of the two Bobbies. At least he did if you listened to one of his speeches that summer.

Below: Tom Finney, always known for his ability to steal an extra yard on his opponents, in a characteristic shot from October 1959. The match seen here was Blackburn Rovers versus Preston North End at Ewood Park - watched by an enthusiastic crowd of 41,000. The goal being scored here by Finney was one of the four scored by his team which beat the Rovers by four goals to one. Tom Finney was famous for being one of the best and most versatile forwards of his era, dedicating his entire 14 year career to PNE. Affectionately known as 'The Preston Plumber' he played 433 times for his home town club, scoring 187 goals between 1946 and 1960. He was knighted in the Queens New Year's Honour list in 1998. He also earned 76 England caps, scoring 30 goals. A true footballing great, Sir Tom was presented with a lifetime achievement award at the Variety Club Annual Sports Awards in September 2007. This marvellous picture was taken by Howard Talbot, from Blackburn.

Right: Another remarkable photograph - supplied by Howard Talbot, of Blackburn, showing the famous footballing heroes gathered at Preston for the Tom Finney benefit match on 26 September, 1960. The Tom Finney II versus the All Stars II. Just look at the players - back row, left to right Jimmy Armfield (England and Blackpool), Nat

was to become both hero and villain in his chosen trade as a professional footballer. His talent was spotted at an early age and he played for England as a schoolboy before becoming a Manchester United apprentice a year after the Munich air disaster of 1958. He established himself in the first team in the early 1960s as a defensive midfielder and soon won a reputation as a tough tackler who was far from popular with opposition fans. Diminutive, lacking front teeth and extremely short sighted, he was anything but a matinee idol. But 'Nobby' won the affection of the masses when he helped England win the World Cup at Wembley in 1966. His jig of celebration, all toothless grin and squint, was featured on the front and back pages of the newspapers. He played 28 games for his country and, after a spell with Middlesbrough, came to Deepdale in 1973 as a player-coach under Bobby Charlton. Nobby served as Preston's manager from 1977 to 1981, during which time he had mixed success. Here, a heavily bespectacled Stiles was enjoying the celebrations as promotion from Division Two was narrowly gained in 1978. However, the club was relegated three years later and Stiles was replaced by Tommy Docherty.

Lofthouse (England and Bolton), Alex Parke (Scotland and Everton), Bert Trautman (Manchester City), Wilf Mannion (England an Middlesbrough), Billy Liddle (Scotland and Liverpool), Bill Shankly (Scotland and Preston). Seated: Stanley Matthews (England, Blackpool and Stoke), Stan Mortenson (England an Blackpool), Tom Finney, host (England and Preston), Neil Franklin (England and Stoke), Billy Wright (England and Wolves). 'What a team - how much would they be worth now'?

Below: Norbert Peter Stiles was born in Collyhurst, Manchester, in 1942. He

NOW THEN!

...the way we were

Each generation thinks of itself as 'modern', at every stage of life and yet we are all relics and momentoes of our own history. As time goes by, we try to hang on to our more modish and fashionable behaviour and attitudes, sometimes with the thought that we can defy the passing of time, despite our constant creation of 'the past' and our own archaeology. Most people, however, enjoy looking back and remembering with affection things done, things achieved and comparing the context of their early lives with

'improvements' made (sometimes!) in more recent times. Things often seem not to be as good as in the 'olden days', but most of the time we are not looking at a level playing field. Inevitably, many of our childhood memories, whatever our age now, are of endless summers and snow-filled winters, a sort of 'local to us' and historically appropriate version of Dylan Thomas's 'A Child's Christmas in Wales'! But for all of us, time marches on and as we get older, it seems strange that we find ourselves attempting to explain to an eleven year old god-daughter that there WAS life, of a sort, before computers, emphasising simultaneously our incredibly ancient origins! Wartime experiences and memories often define generations, although with involvement in more recent conflicts, even this time line has had to be re-defined. The progress in radio and TV development has outstripped most people's imagination and provided a sometimes obsessive and questionable way of 'stuffing' our days. Until the middle of the twentieth century, children often had to use their own imagination, inventiveness and

All the equipment and artefacts used in play were simple, often loud and often extremely irritating in their use and application, but GREAT fun!

Left: In the 1950's, toys were still quite simple, for boys and girls. In a society that still placed the emphasis on women as home makers and 'children producers', toymakers were still making a lot of money from selling pretty little dolls to pretty little girls, banking on their softness for small, defenceless creatures in their own image. This wonderful picture, taken in 1950, shows two such little girls enjoying posing for a 'family' photograph, repeated no doubt, twenty years later, as the 'real thing'! Note the grittily determined, no-nonsense expression of the young lady at the back and the rather shyer, slightly myopic expression of the seated young lady with hair that, possibly, she has spent the rest of her life not being able to 'do a thing with'.!

Below: The influence of Errol Flynn in the 1940's is obvious here in a game involving bows and arrows. His playing of Robin Hood against Olivia de Havilland as Maid Marian, had a ground-breaking impact, for some little boys, that remained with them to their teenage years (and in some cases even longer!). Cinema has always had an influence on children's re-enactment and performance of stories and fables. Certainly children in the 1940's rarely complained about boredom or having 'nothing to do'. They simply grasped the nettle and worked out what they could turn it into and they did it together!

creativity. The streets were filled with groups of children of different ages pretending to be somebody, somewhere and something else. This was fun for most, freeing and gentle in its stimulation and engendered a relevant and satisfactory competitiveness conducive to learning.

Facing page: Outside, including in the playground, improvisation was the name of the game. You didn't need a ball for football - a tightly bound bundle of rags or clothes would do. There were games that matched the seasons, conkers for example. Those determined to win used foul and dishonest ways to convert the simple conker into a hard and unyielding boulder to cheat their way to success! Later in the year it was marbles with wonderful 'glass beads' put to aggressive and destructive use to determine 'top dog'. There were also 'collecting' activities, usually involving cards with familiar faces, often footballers or film stars. Playground games were often determined by gender, with the differences usually marked by the polarising of physical prowess and single-mindedness on the one hand and a softer camaraderie and togetherness on the other.

Above: History does not relate the reason why the front row of this class of children at the Thomas School were clutching dolls, but perhaps they had just had a lesson on how to hold an infant. Whatever the purpose, it was unusual for a little lad to be seen holding the baby, as it were. Boys would be boys and they were expected to conform to the stereotype of being rough and rowdy. Girls were sugar and spice and would nearly always have bows in their hair. When it came to having lessons from the stern schoolma'am, lads would be let loose with saws, hammers and nails during practical sessions, while the future young ladies would be schooled in embroidery, cookery and related homecrafts. They would learn the basics together, but the purpose behind the learning of the three Rs was quite different and was dependent upon gender. The boys needed to be able to read, write and compute in order to become skilled in the art of business or commerce. Their sisters would find the formal skills very useful when reading recipes, writing letters or balancing the housekeeping budget. Even at playtime there was an element of separation. Boys played football and cricket or indulged in fighting games, whereas the girls went in for skipping, jacks or tops and whips.

Right: At one time, Monday was the traditional washday for many. For working class families, the burden fell upon 'mum'. Her role as a housewife meant that the day was spent boiling clothes in a tub and wringing them out through the mangle before pegging out on the line in the back yard. Before the days of sophisticated washing powders and rubber gloves, reddened hands were her reward and yet there were still beds to be made, carpets to beat and lino to wash. The children needed feeding and the evening meal had to be ready when 'dad' got home. It was hard work and there were few, if any, modern electrical appliances or 'white goods' to make the task of running the house any easier. Many families lived in terraced housing, some of it back to back, with outdoor 'lavvies', where you learned to whistle with one foot against the door in case someone else attempted to enter this little smelly enclave of privacy. Many houses still had a tin bath that was dragged in from the yard and filled with kettle after kettle of boiling water before family members took it in turn to soak themselves. This photograph, dating from the 1950's, shows a typical scene from life at the time; families and communities were close knit, sharing each other's joys and sorrows. It was quite common to lend a neighbour a helping hand in times of need and this was often more than just a cup of sugar. Friendships were often formed that lasted a lifetime.

Right: Conditions may have been grim on ocassions but there was usually time for a warm smile and friendly chat in the street communities around Preston. These were the days when people routinely left their doors unlocked - or open, without fear of someone running off with their television. Of course, they didn't have a television, but you know what we mean! These days the neighbourly culture which we used to take for granted has disappeared from many areas and some people seem to know the characters in the popular soap operas better than the people next door. It would be unusual, to say the least, to see a modern housewife scrubbing the pavement outside her house in the 1990s!

Right: Fashion on the beach has surely changed a lot over the last one hundred years. Appropriate beach wear for men and women has moved with fashion. At one time, wool was, amazingly, seen as a suitable fabric for bathing outfits, despite its hideous stretching and shapeless qualities. Topless men on the beach were seen, at one time, as rather racy and promiscuous; yet, how would our Victorian forebears have dealt with the increased promiscuity of the last twenty years, with men AND women prepared to do and bare anything and everything on a beach; they would have been horrified never mind amused! In those days, young women were very bold if they revealed their ankles, knees and arms as they changed, on their parent's insistence, into their bathing attire inside a bathing cart that could be wheeled into the water. Discretion was everything and a lack of it irreversible and so morality and prudence were established and preserved! A hundred years from now, however, we can be certain that OUR successors will look back with equal, if not increased, incredulity at our take on what is appropriate or not to wear on a beach!

Below: Out of necessity, road safety has become a major issue for all of us in our lifetimes and has been written into the school curriculum since the middle of the twentieth century. As we can

see in photographs from the turn of the twentieth century which appear in this book, children played games in the streets and rode their bicycles on the carriageway with little danger to life or limb. With the steadily increasing traffic in the 1930's, safety became an obvious and challenging issue and with accident statistics rising alarmingly the government of the day was obliged to take action. Driving tests were introduced, Belisha Beacon crossings appeared in towns and cities and that well-known bestseller, The Highway Code was formulated and published. After the Second World War, local councils turned their attention to the protection of children, who, at the time, lacked awareness of the dangers that existed in merely crossing the road or cycling to the shops. In this photograph taken in 1950, youngsters are given instruction on a model roadway system.

Stop, look and listen were watchwords drummed into children together with instruction on how to signal correctly and how to use crossings safely. Too many young people lost their lives through ignorance and generally the population were happy to see schemes, such as cycle proficiency, being promoted. In later years, we saw the Tufty Club, the Green Cross Code and, frighteningly, a fully permed Kevin Keegan advising us on why it was NOT a good idea to run out from behind parked cars! Sometimes, it all seemed a little light-hearted, but at least it aided the retention of this information in the heads of children.

Below: When Ernest Evans asked whether it was a bird or a plane up there and answered himself by telling us that it was a twister, a craze was born that swept dance floors across the western world. He also made sure that countless numbers of children would be embarrassed at weddings, 21st dos and parties during the 1990s as their parents risked hernias and heart attacks attempting to twist the night away whilst their offspring raised their eyes to heaven. Evans was a fan of the 1950s rocker Fats Domino and used his name as the inspiration for becoming known as Chubby Checker. Oddly, his first big hit in Britain was in 1963 with 'Let's Twist Again', a follow up to 'The Twist', a record that only became very popular the following year. By 1963, when this couple attempted to keep their seams straight as they girated in the front room to the music from their Dansette record player, Chubby's star had already begun to wane. He switched to the limbo in an effort to promote another dance form, but with limited success. Re-issues of his twist records have enjoyed new popularity in the intervening years, but have only added to the cringe factor for those forced to watch this couple 40 years on as they take the floor to the sound of 'Twist and Shout' or 'Peppermint Twist'. Sit down, mum, it's so gross.

BIRD'S EYE VIEW

The bird's eye view of the town centre was probably taken in late 1947, not long after there was a major fire here, as the Town Hall in the centre appears to be missing much of its roof. Vehicles were using the Flag Market as a car park in front of the Harris Museum, Art Gallery and Library. Cheapside runs down to the right of the war memorial and becomes Friargate further along. Fishergate comes into the picture from the right, becoming Church Street by the Town Hall. The church at the top left is that of St John the Divine, our parish church. Originally the site was dedicated to St Wilfrid, but during the reformation it was renamed as he was thought to have been too much of a confidant of the Pope to be acceptable to the new Anglicans. It was also felt that St John, as an evangelist, was closer to Jesus. Around this time, the old church was pulled down and rebuilt. It was demolished once more in the middle of the 19th century and Edwin Shellard designed the replacement. He had earlier helped build churches in Oldham and Manchester, as well as one in Lytham coincidentally with the same name as Preston's parish church.

The 1965 view of Preston was taken across the railway goods yards. It shows the back of Fishergate buildings and the tunnel under the road that was constructed for the old tramway and provided a connection between the Lancaster and Leeds-Liverpool Canals. Butler Street is to the left and the Fishergate Shopping Centre now dominates this area. St Mark's Church can be seen in the distance, its spire rising above the rooftops. Built in 1862 on Wellington Terrace, it closed some years ago and was turned into flats. The tower to the right of centre with the clock face belongs to Fishergate Baptist Church. This is a Grade II listed building that has stood since Victorian times despite being damaged in 1992 by an IRA bomb blast that was aimed at the adjacent Army recruiting office. The church required more repairs in early 2007 after storm damage to the tower and roof. The railway station opened in 1838 and was extended in 1850 when new platforms were built to give access to the new East Lancashire line. Preston is roughly halfway between London and Glasgow and trains without dining cars on this route used to stop here for a while to allow passengers to use the station's refreshment facilities. By the late 1860s, some 150 trains were passing though the station each day. It was rebuilt in 1880, but its size was reduced in the 1960s when several platforms that served lines axed by the Beeching cuts were removed.

Jane Morgan sang 'The day that the rains came down' in 1958 and the Cascades warbled about 'The rhythm of the rain' in 1963, but there was not a lot of singing going on around the cricket ground and station in November 1980. The aerial view shows a lake where the marl square should be. The camera was pointed from above South Meadow Lane and across to West Cliff, with Fishergate and the edge of the town centre beyond. Preston Cricket Club played in the Palace Shield competition from 1922 as Dick Kerr's, a team from the engineering factory on Strand Road. The side gained immediate success, winning the league on six occasions during that decade. One of its top bowlers, B F Morgan, took 111 wickets at a cost of just 4.9 runs each in 1929, a record that still stands. The club did not return to the league after the last war, but was re-admitted under English Electric sponsorship in 1953.

AT WORK

The United Electric Car Works on Strand Road was acquired by Dick Kerr and Company in late 1917. The Scottish concern had already established itself in nearby factory premises in 1897 making tramcars after expanding its production here from Kilmarnock. During the Great War, the works became a munitions factory and later produced machines that had a direct impact on the war effort. Dick Kerr and Company employed a huge number of women during World War I, with over 2,000 manufacturing munitions.

The 1915 view of the main machine shop shows shell components being produced. This was dangerous work. It only needed a spark from something dropped onto another surface for it to cause an explosion. Workers were frisked for such obviously dangerous materials as matches and cigarettes. Anyone being so foolish as to bring those into the factory would not just be sacked, but face an appearance in front of the local magistrates as well. Many women moved into the areas where the factories were based as the wages were comparatively good.

Strand Road firm was actually called Dick, Kerr and Company, but for many the comma got lost somewhere along the way. It was first known as W B Dick and Company. After merging with Kerr, Stuart and Company, parts of the names of the two companies were retained, though some people presumed that Dick Kerr was one person. A ladies' football team was formed in 1917 as one way of helping boost morale among the work force. Almost every factory across Britain that was involved in war work had its own women's side.

There were drawbacks. Some became known as 'the canaries' because they dealt with chemicals and TNT that caused their skin to turn yellow. Around 400 women died from overexposure to these during this war and others suffered from blurred vision and headaches because of the fumes and the dust. These women were photographed in 1918 working on the fuselages of F3 and F5 Felixstowe flying boats. Over 130 were ordered but only 14 completed as the end of the war made construction of more of these aeroplanes surplus to needs. Dick Kerr's became part of English Electric in 1919 when four companies were amalgamated. The

On Christmas Day, 1917, over 10,000 spectators turned up at Deepdale to watch Dick Kerr's Ladies play their first game. Over £600 was raised to help wounded soldiers. The women continued with the club in peacetime and helped turn the team into the most celebrated in the history of women's football. A game against Everton Ladies on Boxing Day 1920 attracted a massive 53,000 to witness a game at Goodison Park. Fuddy-duddies in the Football Association banned ladies' soccer from its grounds in 1921, a sanction that would last for half a century. Although Dick Kerr's carried on until disbanding in 1965, the great days had gone.

Above: More women, and one or two men, at work at the Tennyson Road Weaving Mill. The decline of Preston's weaving and spinning industry is well documented. From a peak of around 65 mills dedicated to textile weaving or cotton spinning at the time of the First World War, a combination of cheap foreign imports and outdated machinery resulted in fewer than ten mills remaining in operation in the 1980s and only two local textile companies actively engaged in this sector by the early 1990s.

Below right: The treadmill is now commonplace in the modern gymnasium as an aid to fitness and a way of working out that will be of cardiovascular benefit. It is little more complicated than a simple conveyor belt. The treadmill or treadwheel was operated by a horse or ox and worked in a similar fashion to a waterwheel in a traditional mill. Its history goes back thousands of years and includes examples of humans operating these contraptions. Quite often such work was given to slaves or ne'er-do-wells. This idea was adopted as a punitive measure for British convicts following the invention in 1817 by the civil engineer, Sir William Cubitt (1785-1861), of a treadmill that could be used by a large group of men. No skill was required to work it and prisoners could not neglect their task because all must work equally and synchronise their steps. The power it generated could grind grain to offset the cost of providing their food. In the harsh environment of 19th century prisons, the treadmill was seen as an appropriate punishment for those who broke institution rules. Women sentenced to hard labour were occupied on the wheels as well as men. Preston's prison, on Ribbleton Street at the end of Church Street, opened in 1790, replacing the former House of Correction that used the former friary on Friargate. It closed in 1931, but reopened for military use in 1939 and as a civilian prison in 1948. It became a local prison in 1990, nearly a century after the treadmill was outlawed in Britain's gaols.

Below: The construction workers leaned on their shovels as they posed for the camera in 1922. They were involved in the creation of Alston Reservoir, near Longridge. It was heavy work, but at least the men had some assistance from modern machinery. The steam navvy provided the lifting power to load up the railway wagons. The first reference to navvies was made in describing navigational labourers in such terms when canals were first being dug. The term was transferred to those working on the railways, creating cuttings and embankments in the 19th century. Many were Irish immigrants and the abbreviated term was not used with any particular affection. Navvies were regarded as rough, tough, hard drinking men who were best avoided in an argument.

Those employed on the Liverpool and Manchester Railway were paid on a daily basis in an effort to make sure that they did not have too much cash in their pockets at any one time to squander on ale and porter. Meal tokens were also issued as part of the wage, again ensuring that the men ate a proper meal and did not rely solely on alcohol as their inner fuel. The Ruston steam navvy was mainly used in excavating the reservoir bed within the area to be flooded. The material that was dug out was transferred, via the wagons on the temporary narrow gauge railway, to the places where the dam embankment was to be created. The Ruston company was founded in Lincoln in 1875 and, over the next 50 or more years, saved many men from sore backs.

Above: In 1915 this group of ladies, led by Mayoress Mrs H Cartmell, in the centre, helped to prepare food parcels for those who had been captured and were detained as prisoners of war. The Red Cross was given the task of getting the gifts to the soldiers and the knowledge that someone at home was thinking about them helped raise the morale of men who were separated for an indeterminate time from their loved ones. Seen in the Guild Hall, these women were from the middle classes who enjoyed doing 'good works'. In peacetime they would have involved themselves in charitable activities assisting the poor and orphaned children.

Right: Even as recently as 1930, some of the town's lights were lit manually by lamplighters using a wick on a long pole to reach the top of the standard. Some of these men doubled as 'knocker uppers' and were employed early in the morning, rousing workers from their slumbers. It was worth the few coppers that they paid so that they would not be late for their shift. Anyone who was sleeping off an extra pint or two from the night before was in danger of losing a morning's pay if they did not clock in on time. This lamplighter was pictured in New Cock Yard, off Fishergate. He would return in the morning with a small hook attached to the same pole that would extinguish the light. His predecessors in the job might have had candles to light or oil to be set on fire. Sometimes they would come equipped with a ladder when the lamps needed their fuel sources renewing. Some lamplighters also took on the role of town watchman, keeping an eye out for those up no good.

Oil's Well at Ribble Fuel Oils

The past four decades have seen many changes. In 1967 the average price of a new house was less than £4,000 and petrol cost just 27p per gallon. Inflation was running at 2.7% and a brand new Ford Cortina cost only £750!

And in Preston a new business was being established.

Ribble Fuel Oils was brought into being in 1967 by Hermon and Andrea Hodge.

The business has become one of the largest family-owned fuel companies in the North West, built purely on service and good value. It is continuing to expand and has invested heavily in the environmental improvements at its depot to ensure it continues to be able to offer the best price and the best service available today to both domestic and commercial clients.

Hermon Hodge had previously worked for Preston Farmers before setting up the fuel oil distribution business. With just two staff the business first started at Wesley Street, Bamber Bridge, before moving to its present base at 281 Carnfield Place, Walton Summit, Bamber Bridge, in 1984.

Local offices would eventually be opened in Ulverston, Leeds, Liverpool and Manchester.

Today the business has 44 staff and has recently expanded through the acquisition of Leighton Oils in Southport, Geo. Broughton in Blackburn and OSS Fuels in Liverpool.

David Hodge has been President of the Federation of Petroleum Suppliers from 2007–2009. David, the second generation of the family, is Managing Director of the company; Ian Hodge is Managing Director of the associated business, Complete Tank Solutions.

Top and left: *Two early Ribble Fuel Oils tankers.* **Bottom left:** *Where it all began, the company's first premises at Wesley Street, Bamber Bridge, Preston.* **Right:** *David Hodge, Managing Director.* **Below:** *Ribble Fuel Oils' 281 Carnfield Place, Walton Summit, Bamber Bridge premises, 2009.*

T. Snape & Company - a Long Run of Printing

One of Preston's oldest established businesses, T. Snape & Company Ltd, printers, was founded by Thomas Snape in 1858. Those times were exciting ones for England, then at the very height of the Victorian age. The previous year the Empire had suffered the Indian Mutiny, whilst the following year would see the publication of Charles Darwin's highly controversial book The Origin of Species.

For printer Thomas Snape however, what mattered most was to be found not in far off India or London, but in Lancashire. Preston's population was still growing rapidly as it had been for half a century, rising from just 12,000 in 1800 to over 70,000 in the wake of industrial expansion.

From his premises in Bolton's Court, Thomas Snape supplied many of the town's local businesses, councils and health authorities with commercial print, and has continued to do so for over one hundred and fifty years.

At T. Snape, staff have preserved the tradition and skills required to ensure the highest possible standards. Quality is maintained throughout production of a wide range of printed products from stationery to magazine and book work.

T. SNAPE & Co.,
COMMERCIAL
STATIONERS, PRINTERS,
AND
ACCOUNT BOOK MANUFACTURERS
141, CHURCH STREET;
Steam Printing Works :—11, BOLTON'S COURT.
PRESTON.

Sets of Account Books made to order on the shortest notice, in the most approved style, and at reasonable prices.

MILL STATIONERY OF EVERY DESCRIPTION.

Top left: *Herbert Tracey Snape, son of the founder, Thomas Snape.* **Above:** *The notice displayed in the shop window on 141 Church Street when the company was first established.* **Below:** *Snape's staff pose for a photograph in 1906.*

Today the firm is able to produce printed material directly from clients' own disks or via the internet to provide a complete typesetting and print service. Snape's continues to invest in the latest equipment to enable an ever faster service combined with higher capacity and a professional finish.

The firm uses cutting edge 21st century technology and its high standard of customer care has been unmatched for generations.

The first Annual Report of the Preston Royal Infirmary was printed by Snape's in 1870, the same year in which the company also produced the annual report for the Blind Welfare Society: the Society still remains one of the company's customers today.

In the late Victorian era Preston was flourishing. A highlight of those years was the opening of Albert Edward Dock built in 1892. As well as export and imports to other countries there was a considerable coastal trade. Grain was shipped in from other parts of the country and coal from the Wigan coalfield was sent from Preston to other parts of Britain.

As the business expanded, Thomas's son, Herbert Tracey Snape, had joined the firm. On 8 October, 1892, Thomas Snape arrived at work as usual. After talking for a while with his foreman, he went into his office. Five minutes later when the foreman looked into the office he found Thomas dead at his desk.

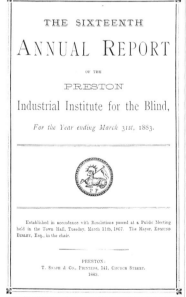

According to the Preston Daily Post of that same day 'An exceedingly painful sudden death occurred in Preston this morning, Mr Thomas Snape, printer of Church Street being the unfortunate victim... it is supposed his death is due to apoplexy'.

Following his father's unexpected death Tracey Snape decided to take on John Sutton and Richard Shepherd as partners. Led by this triumvirate, the company became one of the first steam printers in the country,

and also the first to install Monotype keyboards and casters.

Early in the 20th century several of the company's employees served with honour during the First World War.

Many young men from Preston had joined the forces at the outbreak of war, signing up to join the famous 'Preston Pals', later 'D' company, 7th Battalion, of the Loyal North Lancashire Regiment.

Tragically, during the Battle of Bazentin-le-Petit on the Somme in 1916 some 200 out of the 250 in the battalion were killed. Many other Preston men would not live to see their homes again.

Yet despite the absence of a number of its

Left: The 1883 Annual Report for the Blind Welfare and a Snape holiday notice leaflet from 1939. Top right: The official opening brochure of the Liverpool - East Lancashire Road in 1934, printed by T. Snape & Co.

workers Snape's continued trading throughout the Great War and looked forward to a prosperous peace.

Though peace arrived in 1918 it was not however, followed by prosperity. There was an almost immediate post-war depression in Preston. Following the collapse of the cotton industry in 1919 Preston's economy changed from typical mill town. Diversification included becoming the new administrative centre of the County Council as well as a major route centre of dock, railway yards and road distribution.

As these changes progressed the firm of T. Snape & Company became a limited company in 1927. Tracey Snape died in 1935, aged 54. Richard Shepherd was left to run the company, making Sidney Barker company secretary and later a director.

Richard died aged 79 in 1938 after a sixty year association with the business.

It was during this time that Richard's grandsons, Bernard Swarbrick and Dick Shepherd, joined the firm which continued to prosper.

Remarkably, the business had survived one of the worst economic periods in British history – the Hungry Thirties – whilst many other businesses based in Lancashire in that decade had failed.

The long Depression would only come to an end with the outbreak of World War 2 prompted by Hitler's invasion of Poland. Britain had been promised 'Peace in our Time' by Prime Minister Chamberlain, who had earlier flown to

Munich and famously returned home flourishing a piece of paper signed by Hitler.

Hitler's signature, as it turned out, was worth less than the paper it was written on.

When war broke out for a second time in 1939, all the young men in the company were called up. Bernard joined the Royal Navy while Dick joined the Royal Air Force. During this difficult time Sidney Barker and his works manager Edward Howard kept the business going until Messrs Swarbrick and Shepherd returned from the war. The company was being managed at this time by the late Richard Shepherd's trustees with Sidney Barker as working director.

*Top: One of the company's Wayzgoose. **Above:** A woodcut of the building, still recognizable today. **Left:** A newly installed press machine in the early 1950s.*

Wartime was a period of make do and mend. Neither new machinery nor spare parts were readily available as British merchant shipping suffered terrible losses. Any shipping that was available was needed for food and munitions.

The printing industry was particularly vulnerable – many printing machines were of German origin, whilst imported paper, and the timber it was made from, had previously been imported from Scandinavia, now occupied or blockaded by Germany.

Paradoxically, despite wartime shortages of paper, this was a time when officialdom fell in love with forms and form filling as never before. Though newspapers were often reduced to just a few pages, printing presses across the land clattered away with orders from central and local government as well as the armed forces.

For six long years the focus of the whole country was on the war against Nazi tyranny.

Many of Preston's sons would fall in the course of serving their country. The number of those who would never return home to Preston was thankfully nowhere near as large as it had been a generation earlier when local men had marched away to face the might of the Kaiser's armies.

But that was little comfort to those who had lost loved ones in far off foreign fields.

Just after the war, the company undertook one of its more unusual jobs. Sketches secretly drawn by prisoners of war who had been held by the Japanese depicting conditions in the POW camps were brought to Snape's. The small pieces of paper needed to be ironed out and line blocks made in order for a book to be printed. The book, entitled 'In Defence of Singapore', was dedicated to the members of the North and East Lancashire Regiments who had been captured during the campaign.

In the parish church, only a few yards from the printing works itself, was - and still is - a beautifully bound volume recording the names of 1,201 officers and men of the North Lancashire Loyal Regiment who died in the Second World War. Each name is printed in Monotype Dorchester script on goatskin parchment. The print run was just two!

Throughout the late forties and fifties the company grew despite the long period of post-war austerity, and Snape's became well known for high quality goods and service. It was proud of the number of jobs it was given within Preston itself. For many decades long runs of wine labels for a neighbouring and old established merchant were a regular task.

In those post-war years the company took its employees on an annual day trip, known as a Wayzgoose. Blackpool and the Lakes were among the favourite and most visited places and these days out were much appreciated by the workforce.

Left: Steve, Mick, Gavin and Dave pictured after the installation of a new C.P. Tronic press in 1998. Above: A selection of publications printed by T. Snape & Co.

The company continued to flourish through investment, its first offset litho being purchased in the early sixties. Work on the old machines was becoming too time-consuming.

A booklet of 'hints to authors' that Snape's printed warned them to edit their copy carefully before submitting it for printing because alterations meant laborious and costly work: 'Every single letter and punctuation mark is represented by a tiny piece of metal. The printer has had to arrange these.... He locks the type in a steel frame to make what he calls a 'forme'. It takes great care and skill to do properly. But it must all be undone again before the smallest alteration can be made.'

On the death of Sidney Barker, Dick Shepherd and Bernard Swarbrick became joint Managing Directors of the company, with responsibility for its day to day running. Michael Prior was appointed company secretary. The company's name was by now well known throughout the UK and abroad. In July 1976, Dominic Swarbrick, son of Bernard and great grandson of Richard Shepherd, joined the company which continued, with mixed fortunes to the end of the decade with Frank Ryan as works manager.

By 1982, when Dominic Swarbrick was made a Director, the printing industry was going through great changes. New investment was needed to keep the company ahead of its rivals. After over a hundred years using letterpress, a complete change to litho had to be made. During that year the company installed computerised typesetting. New offset presses were bought, together with modern finishing equipment.

Top: *The Press Room.* ***Left:*** *Snape's town centre premises.* ***Above:*** *Ian Hunniset on the new folding machine.*

Company's plant and equipment . In 2009 Snapes installed its first digital production press taking the company into a new area of print. His son Dominic has taken over as Managing Director. The firm's reputation for high quality print at the right price, delivered on time, was first earned by Thomas Snape and has remained intact ever since.

The company still supplies many businesses in and around Preston with colour brochures, stationery, leaflets, folders and books. Everything is produced under one roof. The firm prides itself on the loyalty of its staff and owes much of its success to the people who have worked there over the years.

Over the next ten years there were a number of changes in management. Firstly Dick Shepherd retired in 1985, after over fifty years with the company. Sadly he lived to enjoy only four years of retirement. In the nineties, ill-health caused the works manager, Frank Ryan, to retire after more than forty years service. His place was taken by Adrian Corcoran who had joined the firm in 1979.

Lisa Swarbrick, Dominic's wife, joined the Company in 1985 and later became Company Secretary after Michael Prior retired. Meanwhile technological change within the printing industry was gathering pace, so yet more new equipment was required at Snape's. Two Heidelberg presses were purchased and Apple Mackintosh computers replaced the now-outdated Compugraphic equipment. New folding and collating machines were installed, and 1998 saw the company purchase its first CP Tronic two-colour Heidelberg press.

The firm became one of the first printers in the North West to install Computer to Plate Technology (CTP). In 2005 it invested in a new B2 Heidelberg PM 74 Press and new folding machine. The following year witnessed the installation of a new Heidelberg QM Press for small run, two colour work. Whilst in 2007 Snape's updated all its PC and Apple Mac computers to fall in line with new technologies. Having printed the brochure for the official opening of the Preston by-pass, the first motorway in Britain, the M6, in 1958, the Company was commissioned to reprint the brochure on the occasion of the fiftieth anniversary in 2008.

Bernard Swarbrick, now in his seventieth year with the company, is the Chairman and retains a keen interest in its affairs and the continuing modernisation of the

Snape's has seen many changes since its foundation, has survived two world wars and numerous recessions and has taken part in seven Preston Guilds. Hopefully, it will see another hundred years. Although production methods have changed the company still prides itself on the quality print it produces and the service it supplies.

Top left: Dave Birtles on the new press. *Left:* Bernard Swarbrick Chairman, (right) pictured with his son Dominic Swarbrick, Managing Director, 2009. *Below:* The staff pictured in 2009.

WH Bowker - Innovation, Performance, Reliability since 1919

The lorry became the icon of commercial haulage as the last century unfolded. The canals were long forgotten and, although rail travel was still heavily used, the improvement in road links meant that goods and materials could be moved ever more quickly and reliably via this means. With the building of motorways in the second half of the 20th century and the increasing volume that larger vehicles could handle, lorries became a vital part of the infrastructure of the nation's transport network and its economy.

The Bowker Group is among the leading heavyweights in this industry. The company has a large fleet of vehicles and trailers shared between operating centres in Preston, Hull and Zeebrugge. In addition to the warehousing and freight handling services that are provided, Bowker also owns BMW and Mini dealerships in Blackburn and Preston, along with one for Harley Davidson and Buell motorcycles.

All told, the company offers a full range of services from the use of a single delivery vehicle right up to packages for major distribution of goods and equipment. It has acquired a particular reputation in the field of transporting dangerous chemicals. Here it sets the standards for others to follow in a tightly regulated industry and has earned a formidable place in the ranks of distributors who are trusted for their reliability, efficiency and attention to detail.

Transporting loads safely and securely across this country and onto the Continent is a job for dedicated professionals and Bowker leads the way in its cutting edge delivery of such a service.

Modern lorries are smart and shiny, clean and powerful. They are a far cry from the chugging contraptions that

first rolled onto our roads immediately after World War I. Although a dreadful experience, war always accelerates technological improvement in certain areas. World War II laid the foundations for dramatic improvements in the aircraft industry.

The 1914-18 conflict, while introducing aeroplanes to a wider world, was particularly influential in opening people's eyes to the value of mechanised transport on the ground. It could be said that we went into the

Top left: *Founder, William Bowker. Above: During the war years William Bowker was taught to drive in a series of short lessons.* **Bottom left:** *The first year of trading, 1919.* **Left:** *A*

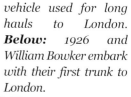

vehicle used for long hauls to London. **Below:** *1926 and William Bowker embark with their first trunk to London.*

the serviceable ones were brought back from France for resale to the general public. Many ex-servicemen used the opportunity to invest their army gratuities into a fledgling road transport industry. William Bowker was just one such man who realised that he could not pass up this chance to be in on a commercial venture that seemed destined for greater things.

In 1919, he began in business from a base at 57 Craig Street, in Blackburn, by carrying fruit from the docks at Liverpool to his hometown market. He continued in a steady way for a number of years until another opportunity for advancement presented itself. It was born out of the misery of the General Strike of 1926 when millions downed tools and the railways ground to a halt.

trenches on horseback and came out of them in tanks, such was the speed of change. What is true is that the horse was still regarded as an important part of our transport culture in the early 20th century, but its day was done by the time the armistice was signed in late 1918.

There was an urgent need for road hauliers to move much needed goods long distances across Britain. William took the risk of committing himself and his finances to hiring other lorries, vans and drivers in order to move fruit and vegetables from Liverpool to London's Covent Garden. His courage paid

Born in 1893, William Bowker was the sixth of nine children. He left school at the age of 13 and went to work in the family fruit and vegetable business. Having spent eight years learning the trade, he answered Lord Kitchener's 'Your country needs you' call and was an early volunteer for the armed forces in 1914.

Top left: *A section of Bowker's Leyland fleet leaving Liverpool with 3,000 cases of oranges for a 6 am delivery to Covent Garden, London.* ***Above:*** *Pictures from the 1930s and 1940s which was a period of building, progress and consolidation for Bowkers.* ***Below:*** *The Bowker fleet in 1954, a time for a new beginning for the company after the Second World War.*

Like so many of his compatriots, William thought of it as a brief adventure. After all, everyone knew that it would be over by Christmas and this was a chance to both serve his nation and have the opportunity to visit Paris. He enlisted in the Royal Army Service Corps and was taught to drive in a short series of lessons that were conducted on London's Horse Guards Parade. Of course, his time in uniform turned out to be a terrifying four years, but he served with distinction driving ambulances and lorries that ferried vital ammunition supplies to the front. This was dangerous work, but he came through and returned home as one of those who vowed to help build a better land for himself and his family.

Thousands of lorries had been built by the government and

off and he was the first to establish overnight trunk movement in the whole of the United Kingdom. William was soon feted as the principal haulier for the Liverpool Fruit Importers' Association.

WH Bowker Limited, as the company came to be known in 1941, developed as a family business. The founder was the governing director and two brothers and a brother in law worked with him. As trade increased and the company expanded, new premises were found at Stansfield Street. Bowkers stayed there until July 1949 before relocating to Hollin Bridge Street. By then, the company was working out of four sites, so the move from Blackburn to a seven acre, later ten acre,

W. H. BOWKER LTD
Hollin Bridge Street,
BLACKBURN
LANCASHIRE
TELEPHONE 50123/4   TELEX NO. BOWKERTRANS 61215

Sole Associates for Lancs & N.W.
FOR
**MAT/ACJ INTERNATIONAL
FERRY SERVICE**

DIRECT DOOR-TO-DOOR DELIVERIES
per TRAILERS, CONTAINERS AND FLATS

REGULAR NIGHT SERVICES
BLACKBURN · LONDON · GLASGOW · BIRMINGHAM

1961

First steps into Europe

position at Holme Road, Bamber Bridge, that took place in 1989 meant a greater co-ordination of the business. There had been much change along the way.

Despite the depression years of the 1930s, Bowker's more than just survived. It was able to progress trade by working for such local companies as Foster Yates and Thom, Henry Livesey, Northrop, Clayton Goodfellows and the Lancashire Cotton Corporation. Help was given to the war effort in the early 1940s as vital goods and equipment were moved across the country by a fleet of Bowker lorries.

Above pictures: WH Bowker have been offering an international service since 1961. Below: Following expansion in the 1960s the company opened a new depot in Hull in 1971.

combinations, authorised dealerships and the opening of the company's own rail terminal when relocation to Bamber Bridge took place. During the late 1970s and 1980s a third generation of Bowkers joined the firm as Bill junior, Neil and Paul came on board.

Although now a major force in the transport industry, the Bowker Group has never forgotten the family business ethic of service, integrity and loyalty. With 150 vehicles and 350 trailers, 500 employees and 400,000 square feet of warehousing it is a large enterprise with a big heart that has never lost sight of its roots.

The postwar Labour government introduced nationalisation on a massive scale. In 1949, it was the turn of the road haulage industry to come under central control. William Bowker had built up a fleet of 75 lorries and an excellent reputation to go with them in the 30 years he had been in business. The newly formed British Road Services (BRS) swallowed up his vehicles and WH Bowker Limited was left to trade just in warehousing. A partial change of heart came in 1953 when the now Tory government decided to sell off one third of BRS in small lots to licensed vehicle operators. William decided to rejoin the industry and recreate a legacy for his sons. Sadly, his return was short lived. William passed away in 1955 and his son, Bill, took over the reins at the tender age of 19. Bill's brother, Ken, would come into the fold as a 16-year-old in 1960. By then, young Bill, thanks to a mixture of grit and determination, had overcome the drawbacks of crippling death duties and a small fleet of lorries that were in dire need of replacement. Somehow, the company survived, though few competitors would have bet on it.

Top left: WH Bowker's relocation to Preston in 1989. *Below: The company's UK distribution service.* **Bottom:** *Bowker's Mini, BMW, Harley-Davidson and Buell dealerships.*

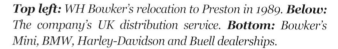

Like their father before them, Bill and Ken had faith in their own abilities and a keen eye for an opportunity. They decided that Europe was ripe for development. In 1961, the first load for Singer Cobble was taken to Holland. The international operation was expanded during the 1960s, with the opening of North Sea Ferries in Hull offering even greater outlets. The first company depot in Hull was opened in 1971, with another following in Zeebrugge in 1976 as WH Bowker International was formed. Dedicated contract hire, providing 'in-house' fleets for manufacturers, was begun in 1978. The 1980s provided more business opportunities for expansion into lorry and trailer

Tom Parker Ltd - Making Connections

The pneumatic and hydraulic specialist, Tom Parker Ltd, is today based at Marsh Lane Mill in Preston, from where it markets and distributes a range of over 25,000 high quality fluid-power products.

From small beginnings in the early 1970s the family firm has grown to become renowned in its industry as a leading distributor of quick connect couplings used in a remarkably varied range of applications involving air, oil, water and gas.

The company was founded June 1972 by Tom and Enid Parker; at that time the business was officially incorporated as Tom Parker (Hydraulics & Pneumatics) Ltd.

Before starting the business Tom Parker had a varied career: he had served an engineering apprenticeship with the Goss Printing Press Company, then worked as an Engineer Officer in the Merchant Navy for nine years. Tom then went into sales, working for Beldam Asbestos Co. Ltd., William Rose Ltd and Lockheed Precision Products (where he sold CEJN couplings) before setting up Tom Parker (Hydraulics & Pneumatics) Ltd with his wife Enid.

The business was started primarily to market the products of CEJN A.B. in the UK and Ireland. CEJN AB is a Swedish manufacturer of quick-connect couplings for use with pneumatics, hydraulics and water.

For the first year the company comprised only Tom and Enid Parker. The business started from the Parker home in Penwortham, Preston. Tom and Enid used their front room as their office and the garage as a storeroom.

Solicitor Mr. J. David Cowburn was a great help, initially confirming Tom Parker's idea to set up the business with his wife, and even visiting Sweden with Tom to help in the initial negotiations with CEJN.

At the outset Tom Parker went out each day selling the products. Enid Parker managed the office and took the orders and enquiries over the phone and on the telex machine (the predecessor to the fax machines), a device which was installed on

Above: Tom Parker pictured in 1978. **Below:** *The company's old premises on Marsh Lane.*

day one in the lounge cum office. The Parkers also had a Post Office Box number for the mail, a simple stratagem employed to give the impression that the business was not based from home but was larger than it really was.

As the stores were initially in their garage Tom and Enid had to measure lengths of hose on the pavement outside to cut them to length. The hose was obtained from local companies and because of the small amounts ordered, was very expensive. CEJN the Swedish coupling company however, gave a good price and helped by supplying promptly.

Many difficulties were encountered and overcome in the early years, not least was getting order quantities of a sufficient size to enable the firm to obtain competitive prices for hoses and fittings bought in the UK. Another issue in the first year was the dock strike in the UK which meant products had to be imported by air – a procedure which inevitably greatly increased costs.

The target for turnover in the first year was £30,000. In fact Tom and Enid achieved sales of £60,000 which had enabled them to employ John Ashurst as their first Sales Representative at the beginning of the second year; he was soon followed by John Neville.

John Ashurst (external sales) and John Neville (who ran the shop and stores), were particularly instrumental in helping the business to grow, both working for the company until retirement.

After two years based at the Parkers' home the business had moved to a shop in Marsh Lane, Preston.

Tom and Enid's three sons, Michael, Richard and Tim, were all involved from an early age: whilst still at school they helped in the production of hose assemblies which were being supplied to clients such as the Ford Motor Company and Rover.

Michael, Richard and Tim Parker are now directors of the company – and their children, the third generation of the Parker family are now involved, working at weekends and school holidays.

The equipment used in the beginning was very basic compared to what the company has today: 'hand swagers' for hose assemblies rather than the hydraulically operated machines that would be introduced later.

Two of the company's main markets today are bolt tensioning, using high pressure hydraulics for both the offshore and wind turbine industries; and pneumatic hose and couplings which go from the compressor to the tools used in production by Automotive manufacturers, the Aircraft Industry and General industry. Couplings and tubing are also used in medical equipment. In more recent years Tom Parker Ltd has become a major supplier to regional distributors of engineering products. To help those clients the company has produced a catalogue of some 20,000 products which the distributors can use as a sales tool.

Key customers include companies such as Airbus UK, most car manufacturing plants in the UK, and the offshore industry, in addition to 'Catalogue houses' which market the Tom Parker Ltd range of products. The firm also supplies medical and scientific manufacturers whose products need specialist hoses and couplings.

Above: *An old company vehicle.* ***Below:*** *A view inside the trade counter area at Marsh Lane, circa 1974.*

As the firm entered the medical equipment market, the 'Hydraulics & Pneumatics' part of the company name came to be seen as too industry-based.

As a consequence, in 1992, Tom Parker (Hydraulics & Pneumatics) Ltd changed its name to Tom Parker Ltd to reflect the company's changing role in the marketplace.

Tom Parker Ltd only deals in the quality end of the market where long life, high efficiency and ease of use coupled with value for money are the main criteria. The company was founded to market CEJN couplings, which were and still are the market leader, and it is therefore necessary to compliment those with products of similar quality.

The company enjoys a special slot in the marketplace not only because it carries large stocks but also because it can give a next day delivery on over 90% of its range. Tom Parker Ltd aims to be the first choice supplier for customers requiring high quality quick-connect couplings and related components. The company aspires to achieve that goal by effectively promoting high quality products from its core suppliers and partners throughout the UK, in order to make them always the customers' preferred choice.

But there's more to Tom Parker Ltd than just quality. The firm has built its reputation on high ethical principles in business: for example it has always been a company policy to pay all its suppliers promptly, resulting in a close co-operation and trust.

Meanwhile the technical superiority of the company's products has been maintained through constant investment by Tom Parker Ltd and its suppliers in developing couplings with higher flows, lighter weight, higher working pressures, and which are ergonomically ahead of the competition. High levels of staff

Top: Inside the works in 1992. **Below:** *A small section of the warehouse space at Tom Parker Ltd.*

training, in the UK, Sweden and USA to complement the quality of the products.

Continuing growth has been built upon a philosophy of providing customers with unrivalled levels of service; through product knowledge, delivery and after sales service. The company intends to continue to expand by following the original concept of working with self generated capital and not relying on outside financing. The business works on the principle of waiting till it can afford the next step in its development: a principle which has stood the test of time.

The company began as a family enterprise and prides itself on still being a family firm with family values despite having grown from once having had just two employees to now having almost 60. A large number of those employees have been with the company for many years. Eleven have been with the firm for more than two decades; a further 18 have been with the company over 10 years, with a total of accumulated experience in excess of 600 years.

Nor is it simply staff numbers that have grown down the years. In the first year of trading in 1972 turnover was just £60,000 and by 2008 annual turnover was in excess of £7,300,000. Stock levels in 1972 were worth just £6,000. Today over 25,000 different products are kept in stock, with a value of more than £1.5m.

The small garage once used as a stockroom has long since been exchanged for 45,000 sq ft of warehousing with products obtained not just from the United Kingdom but also from Sweden, USA, Korea, China, Italy, France and Germany.

Tom Parker Ltd has grown far beyond the early hopes and expectations of its founders. Today the company has achieved a national and international reputation connecting Preston with the world.

Above: *Examples of couplings available from Tom Parker.* *Below:* *Tom Parker Ltd, Marsh Lane Mill, Marsh Lane, Preston.*

James Hall & Co. - A Retailing Dynasty

James Hall & Co. (Southport) Ltd traces its roots back to 1863 when founder James Hall opened a bacon cutting business and retail shop in Southport. The business prospered and James Hall began to supply other shops with his products; so began the business, which was the precursor of today's company based in Blackpool Road, Ribbleton, just outside Preston.

The early business prospered, but the chain of supply needed improvement. This had led to an interest in wholesaling. James wanted to enable other retailers to sell food at reasonable prices in the communities in which they traded. That principle is still fundamental to the company's policy.

As the wholesaling business grew, so too did the need for larger premises. Before the founder's death in 1901 four moves to larger premises, all in Southport, had taken place.

Five of James Hall's nine children entered the business. Meanwhile during the period between 1901 and the end of the First World War in 1918 the range of goods handled had increased, more transportation was required and extra premises in Nelson Street, Preston, were acquired.

Top left: Founder, James Hall. **Below:** J Heaney's store on Fishergate in 1902, the type of business James Hall would be supplying his products to.

Progress would lead to expansion, requiring the building of a new warehouses for Grocery, Frozen Foods and Fresh Foods totalling over 8,000sq.m of additional space.

The Company now serves over 450 SPAR outlets within an area which extends from North Wales to the Humber in the South, and up to the Scottish Border in the North.

James Hall & Co. has always placed all its resources behind the development of SPAR in the UK.

The convenience concept, with SPAR shops trading longer hours and open seven days a week, was adopted by SPAR in the 1980s. The major grocers were quite content with the sales and profits their large scale supermarkets could achieve, and most of SPAR's more direct competitors were lagging behind.

The slogan '8 Till Late' catapulted SPAR to the forefront of convenience shopping with longer opening hours, improved store standards and an enhanced range of stock. All around Britain, independent retailers and wholesalers prospered with SPAR.

*Top left: A 1924 James Hall petrol wagon. **Below:** An etching of the company's Heatley Street premises in the 1930s.*

In 1928 a serious fire necessitated the rebuilding of the Southport premises. In 1935, a Preston company, R. Bannister & Co. Ltd, was purchased and the Company used the former Bannister's premises situated along Heatley Street, in Preston, as an additional distribution point.

By the 1950s, the third generation of family directors - Stuart, Stanley and Philip Hall - had assumed control and the company was operating from two warehouses, one in Southport and another in Preston.

In 1956, with five other leading progressive wholesalers, the company was instrumental in introducing SPAR to the UK. This coincided with the building of a new warehouse in Preston, followed by the conversion of the old depot into one of the first wholesale frozen food depots in the country.

The next ten years saw tremendous growth in the company, due to the combination of the introduction of SPAR and the improved road systems in the area allowing wholesaling activities to extend over a wider area. In 1966 the premises on Blackpool Road, Preston, were acquired allowing the whole operation to be carried out from one centre, and leading to the closure of the Southport site.

Today, the picture is different. Everyone recognises the importance of convenience in the eyes of a customer, the multiples open late and sell petrol, and the petrol companies sell groceries 24 hours a day. Nowadays, the consumers can usually choose between a number of suitable local outlets - and James Hall and Company with SPAR has a single objective, to have them think of SPAR as the best local shopping option.

Throughout the history of James Hall & Company, there has been continuous investment in the development of the independent retailer sector, and SPAR members have been at the forefront of this investment. A typical SPAR shop in the North of England will now frequently offer longer opening hours than competitors, and a combination of groceries, newspapers, beers, wines and spirits, cigarettes, snacks, confectionary and hot and fresh foods, national lottery and other services.

With modern technology and, in particular, the advancement of computer facilities available, not only to the wholesale operation, but also to the retail operation, James Hall & Company and SPAR have continued to make significant developments over recent years. The company remains committed to convenience retailing and will continue to progress and develop the SPAR business throughout the North of England.

From its very modest beginnings James Hall & Co. has grown into major force in the world of retailing, serving over 450 SPAR stores in the North of England. The founder of the Company, James Hall, is never far from the thoughts of current family members who play an active part in the running of the business. They can only wonder of what he would make of the way the business he began has grown and flourished since he created it so long ago.

Above: An early view inside the Bowran Street warehouse.
Below: The counter area of a SPAR store in the 1960s.

In order to keep successfully growing the SPAR business, the company is moving to a new purpose-built site where it will have three times more warehousing space, and a state-of-the art warehouse facility. Moving to this site means offering SPAR members an even better service, and suppliers with improved accessibility to the new site, conveniently located just off the M6 going North off junction 31A.

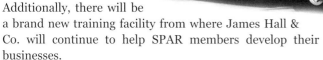

The new depot will also have an on-site shop and forecourt, servicing the surrounding area and traffic to and from the M6. Additionally, there will be a brand new training facility from where James Hall & Co. will continue to help SPAR members develop their businesses.

Currently the Preston-based Distribution Centre stocks over 8,000 items, operating a fully computerised distribution chain with lead times of 24 to 48 hours between a customer's order and store delivery. Voice Picking Technology is used in the warehouse. This technology enables assemblers to communicate with a Warehouse Management System through speech recognition. Assembly team members use a wearable, wireless computer with a headset and a microphone on which they receive orders and confirm them verbally back to the system. The wearable computer communicates back to the Warehouse Management System via a radio frequency LAN (Local Area Network).

The aim is to make sure customers' orders are delivered to them in peak condition. A fleet of dedicated vehicles carries products under strict temperature controls. SPAR members receive one or more 'ambient' deliveries a week, three fresh food deliveries and two frozen food deliveries weekly.

The SPAR organisation is democratic and involves retailers in decision making at all levels through its unique Guild System. Membership, organisation and co-operation form the base of this democracy. SPAR can be seen as a trading partnership between the central distribution centres and the members. Every Guild is based upon the operating area of the regional centres and consists of retailers who elect a committee under the chairmanship of the wholesaler.

SPAR members are served by six regional distribution centres, each operating within a defined territory. The wholesaler and retailers in each territory form their own Guild.

As the Guild of SPAR provides a forum for sharing ideas, it's a valuable source of information throughout the SPAR Group. The Northern Guild has influence on national decisions and offers support to its members and their staff through the Benevolent Fund. The Guild system has strengthened and simplified the communications process from retailers to wholesalers to SPAR Central Office.

In the late 1970s Ian and Andrew Hall became the fourth generation of the Hall family to become Directors of James Hall & Co. (Southport) Ltd. The company still remains a Hall family business: Ian Hall is the Chairman, his brother Andrew is the Managing Director, and Ian's son Dominic is the company's IT Director.

Above: A 2009 SPAR delivery vehicle. **Below:** An artist impression of the new James Hall & Co. purpose-built, state-of-the art facility.

R. Baron Ltd - A Century of Craftsmanship

Training was always considered to be essential to the company's success - a belief handed down from generation to generation. Robert Baron was virtually self-taught, and this is perhaps why he insisted that his sons received the best training available - at the Harris Technical College.

Developments at the Peel Hall Street works included the construction of a purpose built workshop and timber yard, later extended to a two-storey workshop to accommodate the growth in business. That growth was connected with the firm's concentration on two key areas - maintenance and retail shop fitting.

Few Preston people will be aware of the wealth of history that lies behind the joinery firm R. Baron Ltd now based at 1 Wyder Court, Millennium City Park. The exact date the business began is unknown, however it became a limited company in 1918.

Company founder, Robert Baron, had begun carrying out domestic repairs and coffin making around the Deepdale area of Preston, walking four or five miles to each job and returning to his workshop for lunch every day! Robert used a handcart to transport his tools and materials through the cobbled streets to each job.

The firm moved to Peel Hall Street at the beginning of the First World War. Robert Baron continued to run the business himself until the end of the Second World War, when responsibility passed to his two sons, William Albert Baron and Robert Roland Baron.

After the Second World War a more sophisticated approach to retailing resulted in a growing demand for shop fitting

Above: *Robert Baron, in his trademark homburg hat, oversees some local contracts.* ***Below left:*** *A team of joiners pause for a rare photograph at the turn of the twentieth century.* ***Below:*** *This amusing cartoon was drawn by Bill Baron in the 1950s and it depicts his tongue-in-cheek impression of how some customers think a builder's office operates: rows of tradesmen waiting on their hooks for the telephone to ring and a greasy pole to allow them to get to the van waiting outside with its engine running!*

services, and Baron's took advantage of the trend. The ability to work closely with retail customers and produce top quality work was to prove central to the firm's progress.

In 1951 the company received a telephone call from the manager of a large retailer - the job, repairing a broken rainwater pipe, was small but urgent. The request was attended to quickly and efficiently: it was to be the start of a

close relationship with one of the firm's most valued customers - Marks & Spencer plc. What makes this story all the more memorable is that the plumber who was sent out on this crucial assignment was no less that the soon-to be-famous footballer Tom Finney! The Marks & Spencer relationship flourished. It was not long before Baron's was appointed area contractor for Marks & Spencer with responsibility for maintaining seventeen major stores in the region, along with other works in stores nationwide.

Other milestones included the fitting out of the first Kentucky Fried Chicken restaurant in the UK - in Preston – as well as works at Preston North End Football Club, public utilities, several banks, breweries and government departments, and many other High Street stores. The firm's work is still predominantly joinery, but a plumbing division has been operating since early 1997.

Current managing director, Robert John Baron, has firm views about the reasons for the company's growth: "Our customers appreciate the value of dealing with a company which is managed with traditional 'family business values' very much in mind."

"Only happy clients come back; over the years everyone in the firm has worked hard to please our customers - no matter how big or small the job involved - our success can be judged by the level of repeat business we have achieved. One of our strengths is the fact that all the current directors are family members. With a staff of 20 we are able to stay very close to our customers and to keep abreast of their changing needs."

Training continues to be a major strength and it is no coincidence that several of the staff who joined the firm as apprentices have stayed on until retirement. "It is that kind of continuity and commitment that retains as well as attracts our best customers," says Robert John Baron, an opinion, no doubt, that his grandfather would have agreed with.

In 2007 the company left Peel Hall Street and moved to new purpose-built premises in Millennium City Park on Bluebell Way, just off junction 31A of the M6.

After 90 years in the old premises a new chapter in the Baron story began!

*Above left: Tom Finney, of football fame, discussing building and plumbing with Bill Baron and Cyril Naylor, a former manager of Marks & Spencer plc, Preston. **Above:** Tom Finney officially opens Baron's new purpose-built premises in Millennium City Park accompanied by Managing Director, Robert John Baron. **Below:** R. Baron Ltd's new premises at 1 Wyder Court, Millennium City Park, Preston, opened in 2007.*

Bernard Watson - Painting the Town Gold

Can you guess how much gold leaf went into the glittering gold lettering on the front of Preston's Harris Museum? Back in 1986 craftsmen Ken Belton and Roy Lawson took five days, fighting off the pigeons, to brighten up the inscription 'To literature arts and sciences' with £1,000 worth of 23 1/2 carat gold leaf. It took them 100 books of the finest quality double gold leafing to complete the work which would be visible miles away for decades.

The pair were working for the firm of Bernard Watson based at 170 North Road, Preston. The business is one of the North-West's leading signwriting, painting and decorating companies, a local firm whose history goes back to the last quarter of the 19th century.

Established as John Corbishley & Sons Ltd in 1878, the company passed into the hands of the present management in 1979, and now trades as Bernard Watson (inc J Corbishley & Sons Ltd). Since then it has continued to build on its already enviable reputation for the quality of its craftsmanship, professionalism and the excellence of its customer service.

The founder of the business was John Corbishley; his original premises were in North Road where the firm would remain for 48 years. It was not until 1926 that the company would move - though it didn't go far, just across the road, to what are still its premises.

Six of John Corbishley's children followed in his footsteps, and became directors of the business. His grandchildren also joined the company, completing apprenticeships in either painting and decorating or plumbing. In time ownership of the company passed from John Corbishley to his eldest son William who, in his turn, would pass the business on to his son, another William.

On 1st November, 1979 the company was bought by Bernard Watson who had established his own business in 1967. He had served his time with a high class painting contractor in Preston. But not content with simply having served his time, Bernard went on after his apprenticeships to gain an impressive range of further technical qualifications.

At that time John Corbishley & Sons employed eight tradesmen, the same number as Bernard Watson, making a total of 16 time-served craftsmen following the amalgamation.

Top: Managing Director Bernard Watson and daughter and Director Clare Watson. Above: A Corbishley family picture with founder John Corbishley (front row, second right). Left: Pictured, William Corbishley (second row, fourth from the left) son of John, William's son also named William (fourth row, fourth from the left) and George Corbishley (front row, first left) father of Beth Cribbin who still works at the company.

One employee, Beth Cribbin, is the great-granddaughter of John Corbishley; she had begun working for the company in 1975 under William Corbishley the younger, and would continue working for Bernard Watson after the take-over. Astonishingly, more than 25 years after the acquisition of the Corbishley business, Bernard Watson was still employing half the original work force of J Corbishley & Sons, the remainder having left only due to retirement.

John Corbishley & Sons Ltd had been renowned for its ecclesiastical work around Preston, a reputation which was to be carried forward by Bernard Watson.

In 2002/03 the firm won the Painter of the Year award Special Interest category for the fine artwork undertaken at St Mary's of Furness Church, Barrow in Furness. The church was originally designed by renowned architect E W Pugin, and constructed in 1866/67. It took sixteen weeks to restore to its former glory. All the stencils were carefully cut by hand some having eight overlays to get the end result. The job took a lot of time and patience but every minute was worth it.

The company won the same award again in 2006/07 for St Mary's Church, Lea Town, for the restoration of the artwork and the impressive graining work undertaken by Bernard himself who still enjoys using the skill he has honed to perfection over the last 45 years, along side him learning these skills was apprentice Scott Homson.

The award was won again in 2007/08 for the restorative work on the Sodality Chapel, Stonyhurst College, which has had connections with the business since 1925.

Today the company is run by Managing Director, Bernard Watson along with Director, Clare Watson, Bernard's youngest daughter. Clare joined the firm in 1997 and moved the company

one step ahead of it's competitors by achieving the prestigious Investors in People Award. The company has recently moved forward with a new corporate image being introduced in 2008 along with the introduction of recycling their own waste. They are currently in the process of renovating the building that has been their home for the last 81 years and is a landmark in Preston's history.

Bernard Watson Decorators has over 45 years of 'hands on' experience on contracts both large and small, the company can demonstrate a proven track record in a wide range of environments, from industrial and commercial jobs to specialist ecclesiastical projects, leisure and domestic contracts. The year 2008 saw the company's 130th anniversary, and November, 2009, will see Bernard's 30th anniversary at the helm of this long established company.

Above left: St Mary's of Furness, Barrow in Furness, Cumbria. *Top right:* The completed restoration of Sodality Chapel, Stonyhurst College. *Left:* Staff pictured taking part in the Preston Guild, 1992. *Below:* Bernard Watson and staff outside the company premises on North Road.

Whittles
The Jewel in Fishergate's Crown

Many happy couples have come to Preston's premier jeweller in search of a special ring that celebrates the love of one person for another. Seldom are they disappointed. For nearly a century and a half, Whittles has been the focal point for both young and old looking to buy the best. They know that the quality of the goods provided is second to none and the company's deserved reputation is further enhanced by in-house support that always puts customers' needs above all else. Others just seeking a delightful gift or treasured memento will also be more than satisfied.

Although the jewellery branch of Whittles' business includes all manner of coloured, precious gemstones, it is its diamonds that attract the largest interest. Friendly, knowledgeable staff are able to guide customers in selecting the most appropriate ones that meet their needs and are within their means. Concentration on the 'four c's' of cut, clarity, colour and carat is vital in the diamond trade, as each stone is both precious and unique in its characteristics. Of course, Whittles acknowledges that any engagement, eternity or wedding ring is special and every client is made to feel that he or she is too. The individual design of the pieces on display marks out the company as one of the most prestigious in its field, with a distinctiveness for service and after-sales, that is mirrored in its goods.

This family firm has a very strong watch business and is proud of a wide range that includes the finest Swiss timepieces. Rolex, Omega, Ebel, Longines, Gucci and Tissot are names of class and importance that sit well with Whittles. As the official agents for these companies, this Fishergate firm is recognised in the trade as an expert offering a service that is second to none. With a highly prized on-site workshop visitors draw confidence from dealing with highly trained staff whose knowledge and experience goes back over many generations.

*Left: Whittles shop in Fishergate circa 1900. **Above:** A 1937 H E Whittle & Son invoice. **Below:** Whittles' Miller Arcade premises from 1901 to 1967.*

When H E Whittle founded his jewellery business on Fishergate in 1862, it was one of the first retail outlets in the area. Situated further along the road than it is today, it was where Boots would later open a first Preston branch. Whittles prospered by providing a service that was both reliable and gave value for money. The opening of the Miller Arcade in 1901 helped change the face of shopping in the town and Whittles soon moved its business there. A major change was forthcoming when, in 1932, James Rhodes bought Whittles for his son, Roland.

Roland was charged with developing trade even further and he looked around for new opportunities. Rolex, the biggest name in watches, appointed Whittles as its agent. Other major brands followed suit and the company continued to thrive. The Miller Arcade lease expired in 1967 and a move to 111 Fishergate was made. A further relocation to 47 Fishergate, the current home, took place in 1989.

had only just graduated from university with a degree in Business Management. She added further impressive qualifications from the National Association of Goldsmiths and now manages Whittles, with Andrew as a silent partner.

The firm is in the hands of the fourth generation of the Rhodes family and is proud that many of its staff have long associations with Whittles. Some have been there for over 45 years. They have seen many changes in retailing, including a major modernisation at the store in May 2008. Additional safety and security measures were added, so increasing staff and customer confidence in their surroundings. However, confidence in the quality of the stones, the elegance of the timepieces or the sheer quality of the gifts has never wavered. Whittles is still the place that caters for all tastes and pockets.

Above left: An article celebrating Whittles long association with Preston and their move back to Fishergate in 1989.
Top right: Managing Director, Joanna Rhodes.
Right: A view of the new airlock security door.
Below: Inside Whittles new showroom in 2009.

Some four generations of the Rhodes family have been involved with the running of the business. In that time, a loyal client base has been established. It includes regular, satisfied customers who have great affection for a company that has provided them with quality goods that have an air of individuality. Many people recall with affection the former Managing Director, Brian Rhodes, who spent his whole working life in the business. Much of his leisure time was dedicated to his passion for squash, being a county player and international referee and lately taking up golf. His most untimely death in 2001 presented his young children, Joanna and Andrew, with a responsibility they had not expected to come so soon; but they rose to the challenge. Joanna

Kirkham Grammar School

The educational world seems to change every day as new initiatives are introduced, yet a good education is an enduring benefit and some of our best educational establishments have survived the turmoil of changes in current trends whether it be Comprehensives, Colleges or Academies. Kirkham Grammar School is such an institution, enjoying a history and tradition that dates back to the 16th century or even beyond.

Centuries of Christian tradition underpin the education provided by Kirkham Grammar School, which was founded as a charity school in 1549 and consequently celebrated its 450th anniversary in 1999.

Indeed the school's roots can be traced back even further than the reign of Henry VIII's short-lived son Edward VI, to the chantry school attached to St Michael's Church, Kirkham, as long ago as the 13th century. It was there in the church grounds that the school remained until it moved to occupy its present site on Ribby Road in 1911.

Back in 1585, however, during the reign of Queen Elizabeth the first, the Thirty Men of Kirkham, a group which administered parish business, took over responsibility for the school. It appears they did not always perform their duties particularly well for by the early part of the 17th century the school had fallen into disrepair and had been without a master for seven years.

Remarkably, Isabell Birly, a humble alehouse keeper, came to the rescue in 1621 when she presented the Thirty Men of Kirkham with £30 in her apron for the school's restoration.

Although £30 was a substantial amount of money in the 17th century, it was not enough to keep a school running. In 1655 however Henry Colburn, an old boy of the school, left land and a large sum of money to the school in his will, putting it in the trust of the Company of Drapers in London. Then began a long and

cherished partnership between the company and the school which has continued to the present day, though the Drapers surrendered control of the school in 1944 after having endowed it with large and impressive extensions in 1938. The connection with the Drapers is recalled in the School Crest; on the shield are the doves of Kirkham township together with the triple coronets of the Drapers' Company.

Top left: *The school crest and its motto, 'Enter in order to profit'.* **Above:** *The school tapestry showing Isabell Birly in her apron and presenting the Thirty Men of Kirkham with £30 for the restoration of the school.* **Below:** *The school in 2009.*

Independent status ceased temporarily in 1944 when the school became a voluntary aided boys' grammar school. A further major building extension, the Norwood Science Building was opened in 1965, and itself subsequently extended later. In 1979 the Board of Governors took the bold decision to revert to independent status and Kirkham Grammar School admitted girls to become a co-educational school for the first time in its history.

During the last twenty years the school has had a remarkable period of development. Rapid growth in pupil numbers has seen the school grow from a predominately boys school of just over 300 to a fully co-educational school of nearly 1,000 pupils, becoming the largest Independent School in Preston. This development has seen the school develop its own Junior School on a modern purpose-built site adjacent to the Senior School. Pupils are now admitted from the age of three and most continue their education at school until 18. One of the key features in this period of growth was a partnership with BAE Systems, which helped the school design and build its modern Technology Centre, since designated as an International School of Excellence. This partnership has endured and ensures the school has a strong focus on science and technology.

The traditional buildings remain intact with a beautiful façade to the school which provides a strong focus for visitors and pupils alike. The older buildings have retained their impact with a small boarding house still intact with nearly 70 boarders. The Old Hall provides the school with a traditional heart; a setting that is utilised well but which is beautifully set amidst oak panelling and longstanding honours boards. Around this traditional heart, however, has developed a thoroughly modern school with newly developed science facilities, a dedicated drama studio, floodlit all weather surface and recently opened teaching areas incorporating twelve new inter-active rooms. Such modern developments provide the school with outstanding facilities and its pupils with opportunities that are wide and varied.

Following two successful inspections the then Headmaster Mr Barrie Stacey was admitted to membership of the prestigious Headmaster and Headmistresses' Conference in 2000 and his successor Mr Douglas Walker was duly elected to the same organisation in 2002. Recent years have seen examination results and pupil numbers reach new heights and the school enjoys an enviable reputation for its sport, drama, music and Combined Cadet Force.

Kirkham Grammar School represents the best traditions of education in the North West and has stood true to its roots, maintaining close contact with its community. It has, however, embraced the best of modern educational thinking to ensure a thriving school which can now look forward to its 500th anniversary in 2049.

*Top: The school's new Science Centre, Waite Building and Drama Studio. **Above left and below:** Pupils show off their prowess at music and sport.*

Liquid Plastics Ltd - Seamless Progress

Liquid Plastics Limited, based at Iotech House, Miller Street, Preston, is an innovative manufacturer of cold-applied coatings and membranes for roofs, walls and hygiene control. Established in 1963, Liquid Plastics provides systems that are at the leading edge in their field, and are also durable, cost-effective and require minimal maintenance.

The company's extensive product range has been used in projects from the Arctic Circle to the heat of the Persian Gulf, and is regularly relied upon by many major organisations including British Airways, Marks & Spencer, Debenhams and the National Exhibition Centre (NEC) in Birmingham.

With roofing the main market for the firm's products it has sister companies in Belgium, the USA, Hong Kong and Dubai, as well as distributors in over 40 other countries.

The business was founded by Lionel Gorick and his identical twin brother Desmond.

Born in Darwen, Lancashire, in 1927, the Gorick brothers were noted for their inventiveness from an early age, and even by the age of 14 decided they wanted to one day set up their own business.

In 1951, trading from a lean-to garage at their home, the brothers set up the Astral Chemical Company to manufacture a chlorophyll-containing air purifier for use in kitchens and bathrooms. In subsequent years the brothers became involved in a number of business ventures involving plastic, not least Fresconite, a competitor to Formica, and Metolux a high quality aluminium-filled polyester compound for filling dents in motor vehicle bodies. The rights to both these products would eventually be sold off and new enterprises developed.

A novel type of liquid roofing compound was developed in the late 1950s by the Gorick brothers' laboratory – MG Plastics Ltd.

MG Plastics now became a shell company and a new firm, Estacote Ltd, was created in 1963. Two years later it would be renamed Liquid Plastics Ltd. The new business began operations from St Saviour's School, in Malt Street, Preston, a temporary address for the manufacture of the innovative roofing compound. Bob Stanfield, who became Technical Director of Liquid Plastics, was one of the very first employees and would stay with the firm until 2009. In 1966 manufacturing was moved to a disused foundry at Salmon Street, London Road, a site still occupied today.

Top left: Founders, Mr Lionel Gorick MBE and Mr Desmond Gorick. *Left:* Salmon Street, which became home to the company in 1966. *Above:* Extension to Salmon Street premises to enable the expansion of manufacturing facilities. *Below:* The completed renovation of Astal House in 1999 which was officialy opened by HRH the Duke of Gloucester.

The firm became renowned for its seamless, elastomeric roofing membranes, which unlike other products could be applied cold in liquid form and still provide long-term durability.

During the following decade the company prospered and its elastomeric coatings attained world wide sales.

Sadly, the original partnership came to an end in 1976 with the unexpected death of Desmond Gorick. However despite that tragedy the company continued to progress.

Lionel's sons Jeremy and Jonathan both came into the business, respectively becoming Managing Director of Liquid Plastics and its sister company Industrial Copolymers.

To meet increasing demand further premises were purchased at Brockholes View. In 1991 another factory was acquired at Primrose Hill, close to Liquid Plastics in order to meet an increasing demand for resins. In 1995 a large part of the Fishwick Mills site was bought. The five-acre site was extensively developed over the following years, with HRH the Duke of Gloucester officially opening the new office facilities in 1999.

In the Millennium New Year's Honours List Lionel Gorick was awarded an MBE for his services to the plastic industry and to the community of Preston.

By the early 21st century the business was employing some 275 staff worldwide, 176 in Preston.

Founder Lionel Gorick remained with the firm until 2009 when the Iotech Group, the holding company behind Liquid Plastics, was sold by the Gorick family to Swiss company Sika.

Founded in Switzerland in 1910, Sika operates as a global business with a total of around 80 production and marketing companies in over 60 countries. It has had a British division since 1927.

Globally Sika employs in excess of 8,000 people and generates an annual turnover of over 2,000m Swiss Francs.

Sika is active in the field of speciality chemicals, dividing its activities into two business areas, the Construction Division and the Industry Division.

The sale to Sika would open up wider markets to Liquid Plastics and foreshadow global expansion for the Preston firm.

Top left: *Liquid Plastics wins the University of Central Lancashire award for best design and innovation, 2002.* *Left:* *Liqiud Plastics launches its Green Roof System incorporating a root resistant version of Decothane.* *Above:* *Decothane was used to coat the stage at the 2004 Olympic games opening ceremony in Athens - as part of the ceromony the stage was flooded and included a set of flaming Olympic rings.* *Below:* *Directors pictured in 2009.*

Bako NW - Buying Together, Growing Together

Today Bako North Western, based on Roman Way Industrial Estate, Longridge Road, is one of Preston's most important businesses. It has grown remarkably since the early sixties when several independent craftsmen bakers decided to form a buying co-operative called North Western Bakers. Its aim would be to provide all bakers in the area with high quality ingredients, more competitively priced through bulk buying. When regional buying had proved a success, they expanded on a national scale to form Bako U.K.

Five managers, one representing each region's co-operative, would meet monthly to decide which commodities should be purchased, at what price and from whom, so that all members would benefit from the spending power of a national organisation.

Subsequently North Western Bakers' directors (all practising craftsmen bakers) decided to change the name to Bako North Western.

Craftsman bakers buying together, growing together.

Today, the company remains true to its origins, still operating for and on behalf of its Member Shareholders, who are all Craftsman Bakers and Confectioners.

The co-operative began life in a small office in Warrington. The first storage facility was a tiny warehouse in New Hall Lane, Preston. A move came just two years later, to a converted mill in Ribbleton Lane, Preston. However, the building's age and condition meant that the company spent a lot of time and money on maintenance.

On the advice of the Central Lancashire Development Corporation, the company looked at Roman Way Industrial Estate and subsequently built 20,000 sq. ft. of warehousing, loading bays and offices there. Within five years, the company had added a further 10,000 square feet of warehousing. Two years later, additional office accommodation was erected, together with a six-hundred pallet chilled and frozen storage facility.

Adjacent land had also been purchased, which in due course, would double the size of the warehousing facility providing new goods inwards facilities, a test bakery and additional office capacity. Today the company is planning to expand even more. The latest plan will allow for a perimeter road around the entire 6-acre site and provide state of the art vehicle parking and washing facilities, to accommodate the fleet.

Left: *A North Western Bakers Ltd brochure from the 1970s.*
Above: *A company exhibition in the early 1970s.*

Much of Bako North Western's fleet comprises 26 tonne, multi-temperature delivery vehicles supplied by Gray & Adams, of Doncaster, an acknowledged leader in the design and construction of this type of vehicle.

Bako North Western's members are supplied with a wide range of over 2,000 bakery raw materials in ambient, frozen and chilled form. These range from traditional staple goods such as fats, sugar and chocolate, to high quality finished goods.

Handling and delivering are efficient and prompt, managed using Bako's computerised warehouse management system. Appropriate, multi-temperature wagons transport goods to customers in prime condition.

The company adopted 'draw bar' distribution systems, suitable for delivering ambient, chilled and frozen goods to customers. The chilled range includes over 50 different sandwich fillings. Orders for these are taken by sales staff up to midday. They are produced in the evening and delivered to Bako in Preston before midnight for immediate despatch.

Bako North Western now boasts a workforce of 140 and has an annual turnover of £42 million. They also have strong links with Bako Europa, a network of bakers' co-operatives throughout Europe and Scandinavia.

The company's commitment to quality and high service levels is reflected by its continuous staff development programme, as evidenced by their Investors in People accreditation, with trained trainers based on site for

H.G.V., Mechanical Handling and Health and Safety services, which in the future will be offered to customers. Quality systems have been maintained with ISO9001:2000, shortly to be upgraded to ISO2008. Bako also has EFSIS (Higher Level) and gained 5 Star recognition under the B.S.C Health and Safety Management Standard.

While retaining a 'family business' atmosphere, Bako continually seeks to improve its working methods to provide up to date, efficient and cost effective ways to serve its customers. Included amongst those innovative solutions are a computerised 'voice picking' system for the Warehouse, computerised route planning systems, disaster recovery solutions and new call centre facilities.

Many senior managers have retired, having passed on their experience and good practice to those who now follow them. Expansion into commercial markets will provide for company growth, and the current management team is looking forward to the future with confidence.

*Above left: Making deliveries in the late 1980s. **Above:** Part of the Bako North Western fleet in 1998. **Below:** An aerial view of the company premises in the late 1990s.*

ACKNOWLEDGMENTS

*The publishers would like to sincerely thank the following individuals and organisations
for their help and contribution to this publication*

Lancashire County Library and Information Service, Preston District